Leipzig—A Conflict of Titans

Leipzig—A Conflict of Titans

A Personal Experience of the
'Battle of the Nations' During
the Napoleonic Wars,
October 14th–19th, 1813

Frederic Shoberl

LEONAUR

Leipzig—A Conflict of Titans: a Personal Experience of the 'Battle of the Nations'
During the Napoleonic Wars, October 14th-19th, 1813
by Frederic Shoberl

First published in 1814 under the title
Narrative of the Most Remarkable Events Which Occurred in and Near
Leipzig Immediately Before, During and Subsequent to the
sanguinary Series of Engagements Between the Allied Armies of
the French from the 14th to the 19th October, 1813

Leonaur is an imprint of Oakpast Ltd

Text in this form copyright © 2008 Oakpast Ltd

ISBN: 978-1-84677-536-9 (hardcover)
ISBN: 978-1-84677-535-2 (softcover)

http://www.leonaur.com

Publisher's Notes

Contents

Suave etiam belli certamina magna tueri
Per campos instructa, tuà sine parte pericli.
Lucret. Lib. ii. 5.

Leipzig—the Destruction of a City

After a contest of twenty years' duration, Britain, thanks
to her insular position, her native energies, and the wis-
dom of her counsels, knows scarcely any thing of the calamities of war but from report, and from the compara-
tively easy pecuniary sacrifices required for its prosecution.
No invader's foot has polluted her shores, no hostile hand
has desolated her towns and villages, neither have fire and
sword transformed her smiling plains into dreary deserts.
Enjoying a happy exemption from these misfortunes, she
hears the storm, which is destined to fall with destructive
violence upon others, pass harmlessly over her head. Meanwhile the progress of her commerce and manufactures, and
her improvement in the arts, sciences, and letters, though
liable, from extraordinary circumstances, to temporary ob-
structions, are sure and steady; the channels of her wealth
are beyond the reach of foreign malignity; and, after an
unparalleled struggle, her vigour and her resources seem
but to increase with the urgency of the occasions that call
them forth.

Far different is the lot of other nations and of other
countries.

There is scarcely a region of Continental Europe but
has in its turn drunk deep within these few years of the

cup of horrors. Germany, the theatre of unnumbered contests—the mountains of Switzerland, which for ages had reverberated only the notes of rustic harmony—the fertile vales of the Peninsula—the fields of Austria—the sands of Prussia—the vast forests of Poland, and the boundless plains of the Russian empire—have successively rung with the din of battle, and been drenched with native blood. To the inhabitants of several of these countries, impoverished by the events of war, the boon of British benevolence has been nobly extended; but the facts related in the following sheets will bear me out in the assertion, that none of these cases appealed so forcibly to the attention of the humane as that of Leipzig, and its immediate vicinity. Their innocent inhabitants have in one short year been reduced, by the infatuation of their sovereign, and by that greatest of all curses, the friendship of France, from a state of comfort to absolute beggary; and thousands of them, stripped of their all, are at this moment houseless and unprotected wanderers, exposed to the horrors of famine, cold, and disease.

That Leipzig, undoubtedly the first commercial city of Germany, and the great Exchange of the Continent, must, in common with every other town which derives its support from trade and commerce, have severely felt the effects of what Napoleon chose to nickname *the Continental System*, is too evident to need demonstration. The sentiments of its inhabitants towards the author of that system could not of course be very favourable; neither were they backward in showing the spirit by which they were animated, as the following facts will serve to evince:—When the French, on their return from their disastrous Russian expedition, had occupied Leipzig, and were beginning, as usual, to levy requisitions of every kind, an express was sent to the Russian colonel Orloff, who had pushed forward with his Cossacks to the distance of about 20 miles, entreating him to release the place from its troublesome guests. He complied with the invitation; and every Frenchman who had not been able to escape, and fancied himself secure in the houses, was driven from his hiding-place, and delivered up to the Cossacks, who were received with unbounded demonstrations of joy.

About this time a Prussian corps began to be formed in Silesia, under the denomination of the Corps of Revenge. It was composed of volunteers, who bound themselves by an oath not to lay down their arms till Germany had recovered her independence. On the occupation of Leipzig by the allies, this corps received a great accession of strength from that place, where it joined by the greater number of the students at the university, and by the most respectable young men of the city, and other parts of Saxony.

The people of Leipzig moreover availed themselves of every opportunity to make subscriptions for the allied troops, and large sums were raised on these occasions. Their mortification was sufficiently obvious when the French, after the battle of Lützen, again entered the city. Those who had so lately welcomed the Russians and Prussians with the loudest acclamations now turned their backs on their pretended friends; nay, such was the general aversion, that many strove to get out of the way, that they might not see them.

This antipathy was well known to Bonaparte by means of his spies, who were concealed in the town, and he took care to resent it. When, among others, the deputies of the city of Leipzig, M. Frege, *aulic* counsellor, M. Dufour, and Dr. Gross, waited upon him after the battle of Lützen, he expressed himself in the following terms respecting the Corps of Revenge: *Je sais bien que c'est chez vous qu'on a formé ce corps de vengeance, mais qui enfin n'est qu'une poliçonnerie qui n'a eté bon à rien.* It was on this occasion also that the deputies received from the imperial ruffian one of those insults which are so common with him, and which might indeed be naturally expected from such an upstart; for, when they assured him of the submission of the city, he dismissed them with these remarkable words: *Allez vous en!* than which nothing more contemptuous could be addressed to the meanest beggar.

It was merely to show his displeasure at the Anti-Gallican sentiments of the city, that Napoleon, after his entrance into Dresden, declared Leipzig in a state of siege; in consequence of which the inhabitants were obliged to furnish gratuitously all the requisitions that he thought fit to demand. In this way the town, in a very short time, was plundered of immense sums, exclusively of the expense of the hospitals, the maintenance of which alone consumed upwards of 30,000 dollars per week. During this state of things the French, from the highest to the lowest, seemed to think themselves justified in wreaking upon the inhabitants the displeasure of their emperor; each therefore, after the example of his master, was a petty tyrant, whose licentiousness knew no bounds.

By such means, and by the immense assemblage of troops which began to be formed about the city at the conclusion of September 1813, its resources were completely exhausted, when the series of sanguinary engagements between the 14th and the 19th of the following month reduced it to the very verge of destruction. In addition to the pathetic details of the extreme hardships endured by the devoted inhabitants of the field of battle, which extended to the distance of ten English miles round Leipzig, contained in the following sheets, I shall beg leave to introduce the following extract of a letter, written on the 22nd November, by a person of great commercial eminence in that city, who, after giving a brief account of those memorable days of October, thus proceeds:

By this five days' conflict our city was transformed into one vast hospital, 56 edifices being devoted to that purpose alone. The number of sick and wounded amounted to 36,000. Of these a large proportion died, but their places were soon supplied by the many wounded who had been left in the adjacent villages. Crowded to excess, what could be the consequence but contagious diseases? especially as there was such a scarcity of the necessaries of life—and unfortunately a most destructive nervous fever is at this moment making great ravages among us, so that from 150 to 180 deaths commonly occur in one week, in a city whose ordinary proportion was between 30 and 40. In the military hospitals there die at least 300 in a day, and frequently from 5 to 600. By this extraordinary mortality the numbers there have been reduced to from 14 to 10,000. Consider too the state of the circumjacent villages, to the distance of 10 miles round, all completely stripped; in scarcely any of them is there left a single horse, cow, sheep, hog, fowl, or corn of any kind, either hay or implements of agriculture. All the dwelling-houses have been burned or demolished, and all the wood-work about them carried off for fuel by the troops in bivouac. The roofs have shared the same fate; the shells of the houses were converted into forts and loop-holes made in the walls, as every village individually was defended and stormed. Not a door or window is anywhere to be seen, as those might be removed with the greatest ease, and, together with the roofs, were all consumed. Winter is now at hand, and its rigours begin already to be felt. These poor creatures are thus prevented, not only by the season, from rebuilding their habitations, but also by the absolute want of means; they have no prospect before them but to die of hunger, for all Saxony, together with the adjacent countries, has suffered far too severely to be able to afford any relief to their miseries.

Our commercial house, God be thanked I has not been plundered; but everything in my private house, situated in the suburb of Grimma, was carried off or destroyed, as you may easily conceive, when I inform you that a body of French troops broke open the door on the 19th, and defended themselves in the house against the Prussians. Luckily I had a few days before removed my most valuable effects to a place of safety. I had in the house one killed and two wounded; but, a few doors off, not fewer than 60 were left dead in one single house.—Almost all the houses in the suburbs have been more or less damaged by the shower of balls on the 19th.

That these pictures of the miseries occasioned by the sanguinary conflict which sealed the emancipation of the Continent from Gallic despotism are not overcharged is proved by the concurrent testimony of all the other accounts which have arrived from that quarter. Among the rest a letter received by the publisher, from the venerable Count Schönfeld, a Saxon nobleman of high character, rank, and affluence, many years ambassador both at the court of Versailles, before the revolution, and till within a few years at Vienna, is so interesting, that I am confident I shall need no excuse for introducing it entire. His extensive and flourishing estates south-east of Leipzig have been the bloody cradle of regenerated freedom. The short space of a few days has converted them into a frightful desert, reduced opulent villages into smoking ruins; and plunged his miserable tenants as well as himself into a state of extreme want, until means can be found again to cultivate the soil and to rebuild the dwellings. He writes as follows:

It is with a sensation truly peculiar and extraordinary that I take up my pen to address you, to whom I had, some years since, the pleasure of writing several times on subjects of a very different kind: but it is that very difference between those times and the present, and the most wonderful series of events which have followed each other during that period in rapid succession, the ever-memorable occurrences of the last years and months, the astonishing success which rejoices all Europe, and has nevertheless plunged many thousands into inexpressible misery; it is all this that has long engaged my attention, and presses itself upon me at the moment I am writing. In events like these, every individual, however distant, must take some kind of interest, either as a merchant or a man of letters, a soldier or an artist; or, if none of these, at least as a man. How strongly the late events must interest every benevolent and humane mind I have no need to tell you, who must more feelingly sympathize in them from the circumstance that it is your native country, where the important question, whether the continent of Europe should continue to wear an ignominious yoke, and whether it deserved the fetters of slavery, because it was not capable of bursting them, has been decisively answered by the greatest and the most sanguinary contest that has occurred for many ages. That same Saxony, which three centuries ago released part of the world from the no less galling yoke of religious bondage; which, according to history, has been the theatre of fifteen great battles; that same Saxony is now become the cradle of the political liberty of the Continent. But a power so firmly rooted could not be overthrown without the most energetic exertions; and, while millions are now raising the shouts of triumph, there are, in Saxony alone, a million of souls who are reduced to misery too severe to be capable of taking any part in the general joy, and who are now shedding the bitterest tears of abject wretchedness and want.

That such is the fact is confirmed to me by the situation of my acquaintance and neighbours, by that of my suffering tenants, and finally by my own. The ever-memorable and eventful battles of the 16th to the 19th of October began exactly upon and between my two estates of Störmthal and Liebertwolkwitz. All that the oppressive imposts, contributions, and quarterings, as well as the rapacity of the yet unvanquished French, had spared, became on these tremendous days a prey to the flames, or was plundered by those who called themselves allies of our king, but whom the country itself acknowledged as such only through compulsion. Whoever could save his life with the clothes upon his back might boast of his good fortune; for many, who were obliged, with broken hearts, to leave their burning houses, lost their apparel also. Out of the produce of a tolerably plentiful harvest, not a grain is left for sowing; the little that was in the barns was consumed in *bivouac*, or, next morning, in spite of the prayers and entreaties of the owners, wantonly burned by the laughing fiends. Not a horse, not a cow, not a sheep, is now to be seen; nay, several species of animals appear to be wholly exterminated in Saxony.

I have myself lost a flock of 2000 Spanish sheep, Tyrolese and Swiss cattle, all my horses, wagons, and household utensils. The very floors of my rooms were torn up; my plate, linen, and important papers and documents, were carried away and destroyed. Not a looking-glass, not a pane in the windows, or a chair, is left. The same calamity befell my wretched tenants, over whose misfortunes I would willingly forget my own. All is desolation and despair, aggravated by the certain prospect of epidemic diseases and famine. Who can relieve such misery, unless God should be pleased to do it by means of those generous individuals, to whom, in my own inability to help, I am now obliged to appeal?

"I apply, therefore, to you, Sir; and request you, out of love to your wretched country, which is so inexpressibly devastated, to solicit the aid of your opulent friends and acquaintance, who, with the generosity peculiar to the whole nation, may feel for the unmerited misery of others, in behalf of my wretched tenants in Liebertwolkwitz and Störmthal. These poor and truly helpless unfortunates would, with tears, pay the tribute of their warmest gratitude to their generous benefactors, if they needed that gratitude in addition to the satisfaction resulting from so noble an action. You will not, I am sure, misunderstand my request, as it proceeds from a truly compassionate heart, but which, by its own losses, is reduced so low as to be unable to afford any relief to others. Should it ever be possible for me to serve you or any of your friends here, depend upon my doing all that lies within my poor ability. Meanwhile I remain, in expectation of your kind and speedy fulfilment of my request,
Sir,
Your most obedient friend and servant,
Count Schonfeld
Leipzig
Nov. 22, 1813
To Mr. Ackermann, London
P.S.—I have been obliged, by the weakness of my

sight, to employ another hand. I remember the friendly sentiments which you here testified for me with the liveliest gratitude. My patriotic way of thinking, which drew upon me also the hatred of the French government, occasioned me, four years since, to resign the post of ambassador, which I had held twenty-five years, and to retire from service.[1]

From documents transmitted to the publisher by friends at Leipzig, have been selected the narratives contained in the following sheets, which were written by eye-witnesses of the facts there related. The principal object of their publication is not so much to expose the atrocities of Gallic ruffians, as to awaken the sympathies and call forth the humanity of the British nation. Like that glorious luminary, whose genial rays vivify and invigorate all nature, Britain is looked up to by the whole civilized world for support against injustice, and for solace in distress. To her liberality the really unfortunate have never yet appealed in vain; and, with this experience before his eyes, the publisher confidently anticipates in behalf of his perishing countrymen the wonted exercise of that godlike quality, which—*droppeth as the gentle rain from Heaven? And blesseth him that gives and him that takes.*

---

1. R. Ackermann would not feel himself justified in printing this letter, nor in presuming to make an appeal to the British public in behalf of the writer, were he not personally acquainted with the character of this unfortunate and patriotic nobleman, who is held in the highest veneration and respect for his benevolence to his numerous tenantry, his liberality to strangers, and his general philanthropy. To relieve the distresses which he has so pathetically described, the publisher solicits the contributions of the benevolent. A distinct book has been opened for that charitable-purpose at No. 101, Strand, in which even the smallest sums, with the names of the donors, may be entered, and to which, as well as to the original letter, reference may be made by those who feel disposed to peruse, them.

The Battle of Leipzig
14th-19th October, 1813

You know, my dear friend, how often I have expressed the inconsiderate wish to have some time or other an opportunity of witnessing a general engagement. This wish has now been accomplished, and in such a way as had well nigh proved fatal to myself; for my life had like to have been forfeited to my curiosity. I may boast, however, with perfect truth, that, during the four most tremendous days, I was wholly unaffected by that alarm and terror which had seized all around me. On those four days I was a near and undisturbed observer of a conflict which can scarcely be paralleled in the annals of the world: a conflict distinguished by a character which raises it far above your ordinary everyday battles. Its consequences will extend not to Europe only, but to regions separated from it by vast oceans.

You must not expect from me a narrative that will enter into military details, but merely a faithful historical picture of what fell under my own observation; of what my own eyes, assisted by an excellent telescope, could discover from one of the highest buildings in the city, in the centre of operations, in the midst of a circumference of more than eighteen leagues; and what I saw and heard while venturing, at the hazard of my life, out of the city, not indeed up to the mouths of the infernal volcanoes, but close in the rear of the French lines, into the horrible bustle and tumult of the baggage-wagons and bivouacs. We were here exactly in the middle of the immense magic circle, where the incantations thundered forth from upwards of fifteen hundred engines of destruction annihilated many thousands, in order to produce a new creation. It was the conflict of the Titans against Olympus. It is unparalleled in regard to the commanders, great part of whom knew nothing of defeat but from the discomfiture of their opponents, and among whom were three emperors, a king, and the heir-apparent to a throne;—it is unparalleled in regard to the form, for it was fought in a circle which embraced more than fifteen miles;—it is unparalleled in regard to the prodigious armies engaged, for almost half a million of warriors out of every region of Europe and Asia, from the mouth of the Tajo to the Caucasus, with near two thousand pieces of cannon, were arrayed against one another;—it is unparalleled in regard to its duration, for it lasted almost one hundred hours;—it is unparalleled in regard to the plan so profoundly combined and so maturely digested by the allies, and characterized by an unity, which, in a gigantic mass, composed of such, multifarious parts, would have been previously deemed impossible;—it is unparalleled also in regard to its consequences, the full extent of which time alone can develop, and the first of which, the dissolution of the confederation of the Rhine, the overthrow of the Continental system, and the deliverance of Germany, are already before our eyes:—finally, it is unparalleled in regard to single extraordinary events, the most remarkable of which is, that the majority of the allies of the grand army, who had fought under the banners of France in so many engagements with exemplary valour and obstinacy, in the midst of this conflict, as if wakened by an electric shock, went over in large bodies, with their drums beating and with all their artillery, to the hostile legions, and immediately turned their arms against their former associates.

The annals of modern warfare exhibit no examples of such a phenomenon, except upon the most contracted scale. You may possibly object, that in all this there is some exaggeration; and that, if I rate the battle of Leipzig so highly, it is only because I happened to be an eye-witness of it myself; that the French army is by no means annihilated; that in the uncommon talents of its leader it possesses a sure pledge that it will regain from its enemies those laurels which on various occasions they have ravished from it for a moment. You may employ other arguments of a similar kind; but to these I boldly reply, that neither do I consider the French army as annihilated; that such a calamity could scarcely befall a force which in the month of May, after ten engagements, numbered not less than 400,000 men, and was conducted by a general who had already won near fifty battles: but this I maintain, that the mighty eagle, which proudly aspired to encompass the whole globe in his flight, has had his wings crippled at Leipzig to such a degree, that in future he will scarcely be inclined to venture beyond the inaccessible crags which he has chosen for his retreat. For my part, I cannot help considering the battle of Leipzig as the same (only on an enlarged scale) as that gained near this very spot 180 years ago, by the great Gustavus Adolphus. In this conflict it was certainly decided that Napoleon, so far from being able to sustain such another engagement in Germany, will not have it in his power to make any stand on the right bank of the Rhine, nor recover himself till secure with the relics of his dispirited army behind the bulwarks of his own frontier.

Four times had the sun pursued his course over the immense field of battle before the die of Fate decided its issue. The whole horizon was enveloped in clouds of smoke and vapours; every moment fresh columns of fire shot up from the circumjacent villages; in all points were seen the incessant flashes of the guns, whose deep thunders, horribly intermingled with continual volleys of small arms, which frequently seemed quite close to the gates of the city, shook the very ground. Add to this the importance of the question which was to be resolved in this murderous contest, and you may form a faint conception of the anxiety, the wishes, the hopes,—in a word, of the cruel suspense which pervaded every bosom in this city.

Marmont
Early October

To enable you to pursue the train of events, as far as I was capable of informing myself respecting them, I will endeavour to relate them as they occurred. It was not till the arrival of Marshal Marmont with his corps of the army in this neighbourhood that any idea of the probability of a general engagement at Leipzig began to be entertained. That circumstance happened in the beginning of October. These guests brought along with them every species of misery and distress, which daily increased in proportion as those hosts of destroyers kept gradually swelling into a large army. They were joined from time to time by several other corps; the city was nearly surrounded by bivouacs; and, gracious God! what proceedings! what havoc!—We had frequently been informed that all Saxony, from Lusatia to the Elbe, resembled one vast desert, where nothing was to be seen but towns laid waste and plundered, villages reduced to ashes, naked and famishing inhabitants;—that there was no appearance of any other living creature; nay, not even a trace of vegetation remaining.

These accounts we naturally regarded as exaggerations, little imagining that in a short time we should have to give to our distant friends the same details of horror respecting our own vicinity. Too true it is that no nation has made such progress in the art of refinement, and is so ingenious in devising infernal torments, as that, which, under the name of allies and protectors, has made us so inexpressibly wretched. Ever since the battle of Lützen, Leipzig had been one of the principal resources of the grand French army, and they showed it no mercy. Numberless hospitals transformed it into one great infirmary; many thousands of troops, quartered in the habitations of the citizens, one prodigious *corps de garde*; and requisitions of meat, bread, rice, brandy, and other articles, one vast poor-house, where the indigent inhabitants were in danger of starving. But for this well-stored magazine, the great French army had long since been obliged to abandon the Elbe.

No wonder then that this point should have been guarded with the utmost care. It required commissaries and inspectors, such as those who had the control over our store-houses and granaries, to complete the master-piece, to reduce that Leipzig, which had once patiently sustained, without being entirely exhausted, the burdens of a war that lasted seven years—to reduce it, I say, in six months, to so low an ebb, that even the opulent were in danger of perishing with hunger; that reputable citizens could no longer procure the coarsest fare; and that, though their hearts overflowed with pity and compassion, they were absolutely incapable of affording the slightest relief, not so much as a crust of bread, to the sick and wounded soldier. It is impossible to give you any idea of the dexterity and rapidity with which the French soldiers will so totally change the look of a village, a field, or a garden, that you shall not know it again, how well soever you may have been acquainted with it before. Such was the fate of Leipzig, and of the beautiful environs of our inner city-walls.

You must know that the bread and forage wagons of a

great French army are destined merely, as they pass through the villages, to receive the stores collected from all the barns, cellars, lofts, and stables, which are taken by force from the wretched husbandman, who is beaten, cut, and mangled, till he puts-to his last horse, and till he carries his last sheaf of corn and his last loaf of bread to the next bivouac; and then he may think himself fortunate, if he is suffered to return home without horses or wagon, and is not compelled to accompany the depredators many miles without sustenance of any kind. In all other armies, whether Russians, Prussians, Austrians, or Swedes, when the troops are not drawn out in line of battle opposite to the enemy, in which case it is necessary to send back the carriages into the rear, care is always taken that wagons with bread and forage, and herds of cattle, shall follow the marching columns. Whenever the army halts, magazines are immediately established; and, if even the stores necessary for it are required at the cost of the country, this case bears no comparison with that where every attendant on the wagon-train is at full liberty to pillage till his rapacity is satisfied. Woe to the country where, as in our's, hundreds of thousands of such commissaries are allowed to exercise their destructive office at discretion!

Ask the inhabitants of more than twenty villages round Leipzig, and many hundred others at a greater distance, which certainly fared no better, what soldiers they were who carried off roofs, doors, windows, floors, and every kind of household furniture and agricultural implements, and threw them like useless lumber into the watch-fires?— Ask those unfortunates what soldiers they were who pillaged barns and cellars, and ransacked every corner of the houses; who tore the scanty clothes from the backs of the poorest class; who broke open every box and chest, and who searched every dunghill, that nothing might escape them?—They will tell you that it was the so highly vaunted

French guards, who always led the way, and were the instructors of their comrades.

It is a great misfortune for a country when, in time of war, the supply of the troops is left to themselves by the military authorities, and when that supply is calculated only from one day to another; but this calamity has no bounds when they are French troops who attack your stores. It is not enough for them to satisfy the calls of appetite; every article is an object of their rapacity: nothing whatever is left to the plundered victim. What they cannot cram into their knapsacks and *cartouche* boxes is dashed in pieces and destroyed. Of the truth of this statement the environs of Leipzig might furnish a thousand proofs.

The most fortunate of the inhabitants were those who in good time removed their stores and cattle to a place of safety, and left their houses to their fate. He who neglected this precaution, under the idea that the presence of the owner would be sufficient to restrain those locusts, of course lost his all. No sooner had he satisfied one party than another arrived to renew the demand; and thus they proceeded so long as a morsel or a drop was left in the house. When such a person had nothing more to give, he was treated with the utmost brutality, till at length, stripped of all, he was reluctantly compelled to abandon his home. If you should chance to find a horse or a cow, here and there, in the country round our city, imagine not that the animal was spared by French generosity:—no such thing! the owner must assuredly have concealed it in some hiding-place, where it escaped the prying eyes of the French soldiers. Nothing—absolutely nothing—was spared; the meanest bedstead of the meanest beggar was broken up as well as the most costly furniture from the apartments of the opulent.

After they had slept upon the beds in the bivouacs, as they could not carry them away, they ripped them open, consigned the feathers to the winds, and sold the bed-clothes and ticking for a mere trifle. Neither the ox, nor the calf but two days old; neither the ewe, nor the lamb scarcely able to walk; neither the brood-hen, nor the tender chicken, was spared. All were carried off indiscriminately; whatever had life was slaughtered; and the fields were covered with calves, lambs, and poultry, which the troops were unable to consume. The cattle collected from far and near were driven along in immense herds with the baggage. Their cries for food in all the high roads were truly pitiable.

Often did one of those wretches drive away several cows from the out-house of a little farmer, who in vain implored him upon his knees to spare his only means of subsistence, merely to sell them before his face for a most disproportionate price. Hay, oats, and every species of corn, were thrown unthreshed upon the ground, where they were consumed by the horses, or mostly trampled in the dirt; and if these animals had stood for some days in the stable, and been supplied with forage by the peasant, the rider had frequently the impudence to require his host to pay for the dung. Woe to the field of cabbages, turnips, or potatoes, that happened to lie near a bivouac! It was covered in a trice with men and cattle, and in twenty-four hours there was not a plant to be seen. Fruit-trees were cut down and used for fuel, or in the erection of sheds, which were left perhaps as soon as they were finished.

Though Saxony is one of the richest and most fertile provinces of Germany, and the vicinity of Leipzig has been remarkable for abundance, yet it cannot appear surprising, that, with such wanton waste, famine, the most dangerous foe to an army, should have at length found its way into all the French camps. Barns, stables, and lofts, were emptied; the fields were laid bare; and the inhabitants fled into the woods and the towns. Bread and other provisions had not been seen in our markets for several days, and thus it was now our turn to endure the pressure of hunger. It was a fortunate circumstance that many families had laid in a quantity of potatoes, which indeed might yet be purchased, though at an exorbitant price. The bakers of this place were obliged to work up the small stock of flour in their possession for the use of the troops; and all other persons were driven from the doors by the guards with the butt-ends of their muskets; though the citizen who came in quest of bread had perhaps twenty men quartered upon him, who all expected him to find wherewith to satisfy their craving appetites.

Such was what might be termed the prologue to the grand tragedy which was about to be performed in an amphitheatre of many square miles, and to the catastrophe of which we looked forward with an anxiety that had risen to so high a pitch, because, in case of the longer continuance of this state of things, our own annihilation might be hourly expected.

The Armies Approach
14th October

That the grand armies of the allies were approaching
Leipzig, on every side, we had heard through several private channels. Napoleon had quitted Dresden, which he
had been compelled to abandon almost solely by the want
of all the means of subsistence. We were long uncertain
respecting his route, and so perhaps was he himself at first.
Many, who were qualified to form a judgment respecting
military operation's, were of opinion that he would make
a push with his whole force upon Berlin and the Oder.
They supposed that those parts were not sufficiently covered, and considered the fortresses on the Elbe as his *point
d'appui* in the rear. This opinion, however, seemed to lose
much of its probability, as other French corps, under Ney,
Regnier, Bertrand, and Marmont, kept arriving here, and
were afterwards joined by that of Augereau. We had received authentic information that Prince Schwarzenberg
had already advanced to Altenburg with the grand combined army of Austria, Russia, and Prussia; and also that the
Crown-prince of Sweden had his head-quarters at Zörbig.
Upon the whole, however, our intelligence was unsatisfac-
tory. For several days (that is to say, from the 10th) it was
reported that the emperor of the French would certainly

remove his head-quarters hither; that he had taken the road to Wurzen, and was coming by way of Duben.

This account was confirmed by several detachments of the French guard. It is universally known that this general preferably chooses those days on which he founds his claim to glory, in order to distinguish them by new achievements. His proximity to us, and the approaching 14th of October,[2] strengthened the anticipation of some important event in our neighbourhood. The light troops of the allies, whom we took for the advanced guard of the Crown-prince of Sweden, were distinctly to be seen from the steeples of the city, on the north side of it, towards Breitenfeld and Lindenthal. Daily skirmishes ensued, and wounded French were hourly brought in. The bustle in the city increased; the king of Naples had arrived, and fixed his head-quarters at Konnewitz. Innumerable generals and staff-officers filled all the houses. Not a moment's rest was to be had; all were in bivouac. They seemed wholly ignorant of the motions of the allies; for the same troops who went out at one gate often returned before night at another; so that there was an incessant marching in and out at all the four principal avenues of the city. These movements of cavalry, infantry, and carriages, ceased not a moment even during the night It was very rarely that a troop of cavalry, sent out upon patrol or picket duty, returned without having lost several men and horses, who were invariably, according to their report, kidnapped by the Cossacks. Upon the whole, all the troops with whom the French had any rencounters were called by them *Cossacks*—a name which I have heard them repeat millions of times, and to which they never failed to add, that "the fellows had again set up a devilish hurrah."

The Cossacks are indisputably the troops of whom the French are most afraid. With them, therefore, all the light

2. The 14th of October is the anniversary of the battles of Ulm and of Jena.

cavalry who come upon them unawares are sure to be Cossacks. In revenge for the many annoyances which they were incessantly suffering from these men, they applied to them the opprobrious epithet of *brigands*. Often did I take pains to convince them that troops who were serving their legitimate sovereign, and fighting under the conduct of their officers, could not be termed *banditti*; my representations had no effect,—they were determined to have some satisfaction for their disappointment in a thousand attempts to master such enemies. Their vanity was far too great to suffer them to do justice to those warriors; and they never would admit what thousands had witnessed, namely, that thirty French horse had frequently run away from two Cossacks.

If Napoleon had twenty thousand Russian Cossacks in his service, the French journalists and editors of newspapers would scarcely be able to find terms strong enough to extol these troops; and the French have just reason to rejoice that the emperor Alexander has no such rivals of their government in his pay, otherwise we should hear of their exploits only, and the vaunted French horse-guards would long since have sunk into oblivion.

All the preparations that were making now evidently denoted that we were on the eve of important events. The French corps had already ranged themselves in a vast semicircle, extending from north to east, and thence to south-west. The country towards Merseburg and Weissenfels seemed to be merely observed. For this purpose the eminences beyond the village of Lindenau were occupied. Here the access to the city is the most difficult, a causeway only leading to it in this direction.

The country on the right and left consists of swampy meadows and wood-land, everywhere intersected by ditches and muddy streams. If you inquired of the French officers what might be the total strength of their army about Leipzig, their statements were so various, that it was impossible to fix with the least confidence upon any number as a medium. By what standard, indeed, can you judge of a force rated by some at 150,000, by others at 400,000 men? They unanimously agreed, on the other hand, that the allies would be opposed by fifteen corps, exclusively of the guards.

I had an opportunity of forming a tolerably correct estimate of one division of Marmont's corps, which consisted at the utmost of 4000, so that the whole might amount to 12,000 men; and it was one of those which, in comparison of others, had sustained the least loss. Even that of Augereau, which was incontestably the most complete, as it had just come out of cantonments, was computed at scarcely 15,000 men. If, then, we take 10,000 for the average, the total amount of the French armies collected near Leipzig, as the wrecks only of several were then remaining, can scarcely have reached 170,000, even including the guards. Such a force, however, commanded by so many generals who had heretofore been acknowledged the ablest in Europe, together with more than 600 pieces of artillery, was still fully sufficient to make itself respected, and even feared, by an enemy of double its number.

One single species of troops alone was below mediocrity:—the cavalry, both in regard to the horses and the men, the former from weakness and want of sustenance, and the latter from ignorance of their business. With the force of the allies we are yet unacquainted, but at all events they must have been more numerous.

The 14th of October at length dawned. It had preceded by several rainy days; but this was merely lowering. The cannon thundered at intervals towards Liebertwolkwitz. In the forenoon wounded French, chiefly cavalry, kept coming in singly. With whom they had been engaged they knew not—*Cossacks*, of course. We looked forward with certainty to a general engagement. It became every hour more dangerous for the inquisitive to venture out or in at the gates. There was no end to the marching of horse and foot and the rolling of carriages; at every ten paces you met in all directions with *corps de garde*, by whom every non-military person without distinction was ordered back, sometimes with fair words, and at others with rudeness. Several couriers had been sent forward to announce the speedy arrival of the King of Saxony and Napoleon.

The Battle Commences

The hero of the age, as he has been styled, actually came about noon, not, as we anticipated, by the Dresden road, but by that from Berlin. He passed hastily through the city, and out at the farthest Grimma gate, attended by some battalions and squadrons of his guards. A camp-chair and a table were brought in all haste, and a great watch-fire kindled in the open field; not far from the gallows. The guards bivouacked on the right and left. The emperor took possession of the head-quarters prepared for him, which were anything but magnificent, being surrounded only by the relics of the stalks and leaves of the cabbages consumed by his soldiers, and other matters still more offensive. The table was instantly covered with maps, over which the emperor pored most attentively for a considerable time.

Of what was passing around him he seemed not to take the smallest notice. The spectators, of whom I was one, crowded pretty close about him. On occasion of his visit to the city, a few months before, the French had discovered that the people of Leipzig were not so malicious as they had been represented, but tolerably good-natured creatures. They were therefore allowed to approach unobstructed within twenty paces. A long train of carriages from the Wurzen road, the cracking of the whips of the postilions, together with a great number of horse-soldiers and tall grenadiers, announced the arrival of another distinguished personage, and called the attention of the bystanders that way. It was the King of Saxony, with his guards and retinue. He alighted, and a kind salutation ensued between him and his august ally. The king soon afterwards mounted a horse, and thus proceeded into the city.

Napoleon meanwhile remained where he was. He sometimes rose from his seat, went up to the watch-fire, held his hands over it, rubbed them, and then placed them behind him, whilst with his foot he pushed the wood, consisting of dry boards and rafters from the nearest houses, into the flame, to make it burn more fiercely. At the same time he very frequently took snuff, of which he seemed to have but a small quantity left in his gold box. At last he scraped together what was left with his finger, and poured it out upon his hand.

When all was gone, he opened the box several times and smelt to it, without applying to any of the marshals and generals around him to relieve his want. As the discharges of artillery towards Probstheide grew more and more general and alarming, and the wounded kept returning in continually increasing numbers, I was rather surprised that the commander should, on this occasion, contrary to his usual custom, quietly remain so far from the field of battle, which was near ten miles distant, apparently without giving himself the least concern about the event.

It was about four in the afternoon when one of his aid-de-camps came at full speed from the city, and made a report. The drums instantly beat to arms, and the divisions of the guards broke up. The emperor immediately mounted his horse, and followed them. He directed his course towards the Kohlgärten,[3] leaving the field of battle on the right. I soon perceived the cause of this movement: the message informed him of the arrival of the whole of his guards, for whom he had been waiting. They came from Düben, entering by the Halle gate, and now made a counter-march upon Dresden. When I beheld their endless files and cannon without number pouring out of the city, I certainly gave up the allies for lost. I was thoroughly convinced that Napoleon had no other plan than to strike off to the right behind the Kohlgärten, with his new army, and, proceeding from Stötteritz, to turn his enemies on the right flank, and, as he had often done before, to attack and annihilate them. I was however egregiously mistaken. The emperor went with his retinue scarcely a thousand paces, to the first houses of the Kohlgärten, where he took up his quarters, and quietly passed the night.

---

3. What is yet called the Kohlgärten was formerly gardeners' ground for the supply of the city, and is now converted into a fashionable village, consisting chiefly of the country-houses of merchants; and where is also a public garden for the recreation of the citizens.

Within & Without the City
15th October

The guards and the whole train likewise stopped in that neighbourhood, and there bivouacked. It grew dark. The palisades at the gate had left but a narrow passage, through which troops and artillery kept pouring without intermission. People on horseback and on foot, who wanted to return into the city, had been already detained for several successive hours; the crowd every moment increased, and with it the danger. To seek another entrance was impracticable, as a person would run the risk of being detained by the thousands of pickets, and shot, or at least dragged to the filthiest bivouacs. The night was dark as pitch, and no hope left of getting home. It rained fast, and not a corner was to be found where you might take shelter. I was in the midst of more than a thousand horses, which threatened every moment to trample me under their feet. Fortunately for me, they were all tolerably quiet.

The thunder of the artillery had long ceased; but, had it even continued, it could not possibly have been heard amidst the rattling of carriages and cannon; the shouts of soldiers and officers, as sometimes cavalry, at others infantry, wanted to pass first; the incessant cursing, cracking, pushing, and thrusting. Never while I live shall I witness such a scene of confusion, of which indeed it is impossible to convey any conception. It continued without intermission from four in the afternoon till twelve at night, so that you may figure to yourself the disagreeable situation in which I was placed.

No sooner had the first columns arrived at their bivouacs in the neighbouring villages, than a thousand messengers came to announce the intelligence in a way that sufficiently proved what unwelcome visitors they were. Weeping mothers with beds packed up in baskets, leading two or three stark-naked children by the hand, and with perhaps another infant at their back; fathers seeking their wives and families; children, who had lost their parents in the crowd trucks with sick persons forcing their way among the thousands of horses; cries of misery and despair in every quarter:—such were the heralds that most feelingly proclaimed the presence of the warriors who have been celebrated in so many regions, and whose imposing appearance has been so often admired, all these unfortunates crowded into the filthy corner formed by the old hospital and the wall at the Kohlgärten-gate. Their cries and lamentations were intermingled with the moans and groans of the wounded who were going to the hospitals, and who earnestly solicited bread and relief.

A number of French soldiers, probably such as had loitered in the rear, searched every basket and every pocket for provisions. They turned without ceremony the sleeping infants out of the baskets, and cared not how the enraged mothers lacerated their faces in return. The scenes of horror changed so quickly, that you could not dwell more than half a minute upon any of them. The tenderest heart became torpid and insensible. One tale of woe followed on the heels of another:

"Such a person too has been plundered!"

"Such an one's house has been set on fire!"

"This man is cut in pieces; that has been transfixed with the bayonet!"

"Those poor creatures are seeking their children!"

These were the tidings brought by every new fugitive. If you asked the French when the march would be over, you received the consolatory answer—"Not before six o'clock in the morning."

During the night the sound of drums and trumpets incessantly announced the arrival of fresh regiments. At length, about midnight, the bustle somewhat subsided, at least so far as regarded the marching of troops. I now seized the favourable moment, and felt myself as it were a new creature; when, having made my way through the crowd of horses with extraordinary courage and dexterity, I once more set foot in the city. *Thus the morning and the evening completed the first day of horror.*

Notwithstanding the unpleasant circumstances in which my curiosity had involved me on the preceding day, I had in fact seen and heard nothing as far as related to my principal object. It was no battle, but merely an indecisive, though warm, affair. The first act of the piece concluded with aft illumination extending farther than the eye could reach, and occasioned by the innumerable watch-fires which were kindled in every quarter, and gradually spread farther and farther, as the lines of the bivouacking army were lengthened by the arrival of fresh columns. By way of variety, the flames rising from a number of burning houses in the distance formed as it were points of repose.

Scarcely was the night over when all eyes and ears were on the alert, in expectation that the sanguinary scene would commence with the morning's dawn. All, however, remained quiet. People, therefore, again ventured abroad, and there thought themselves more secure than the preceding day, because they might the more easily avoid the danger while at a distance-than they could have done the night before. It required, to be sure, considerable strength of nerves not to be shocked at the spectacles which every where presented themselves. Many dead bodies of soldiers, who had come sick into bivouac, lay naked in the fields and upon the roads. The heirs had taken especial care to be on the spot at the moment of their decease, to take possession of all that the poor wretches had to bequeath.

The mortality among the horses had been still greater: you met with their carcasses almost at every step; and, which way soever you turned your eyes, you beheld a still greater number which Death had so firmly seized in his iron grasp, that they inclined their heads to the ground, and fell, in a few minutes, to rise no more! Scarcely was there sufficient room on the high road for a slender pedestrian to find a passage. All the fields were covered with troops and baggage. Even on the place of execution they had erected bivouacs, and not the most inconvenient, because they were there less crowded than in other places. Except single musket-shots, nothing was to be heard but incessant cries of *Serrez! Serrez!* (Closer! Closer!)—The dice yet lay in the box, and were not destined to be thrown that day. It was probably spent in reconnoitring, in order to make up the parties for the grand game in which empires were the stake. The preparations for the defence of the city became more serious and alarming. The exterior avenues had been previously palisaded, and provided with *chevaux de frise*; but the greater part of them were completely closed up. Loop-holes were formed in every wall, and *tirailleurs* posted behind them. In every garden and at every hedge you stumbled upon pickets.

As the inner town is better secured by its strong walls against a first onset, they contented themselves there with sawing holes in the great wooden gates, for the purpose of firing through them. Everything denoted the determination not to spare the city in the least, however unfit in itself for a point of defence. The only circumstance calculated to tranquillize the timid was the presence of our king, for whom, at any rate, Napoleon could not but have some respect.

As there was no appearance of gleaning much information abroad, I now sought a wider prospect upon a steeple.

So much I had ascertained from all accounts, that it was principally the Austrians who had been engaged the preceding day. Some hundreds of prisoners had been brought in; the churchyard had been allotted to these poor fellows for their abode, probably that they might study the inscriptions on the grave-stones, and thus be reminded of their mortality. Nothing was given them to eat, lest they should be disturbed in these meditations. So far as the telescope would command were to be seen double and triple lines, the end of which the eye sought in vain. The French army stretched in a vast semicircle from Paunsdorf to Probstheide, and was lost in the woods of Konnewitz. It occupied therefore a space of more than one German mile (five English miles). Behind all these lines appeared reserves, who were posted nearer to the city. On this side the main force seemed to be assembled.

Towards the north and west the ranks were more broken and detached. Of the armies of the allies, only some divisions could yet be discerned. The Cossacks were plainly distinguished at a distance of two leagues. They had the boldness to venture within musket-shot of the French lines, alight, thrust their pikes into the ground, and let their horses run about. The King of Saxony himself witnessed their audacity whilst in the midst of the French army, about half a league from Leipzig. A number of these men came unawares upon him; and a Saxon officer, with eighty horse, was obliged to face about against them, till the king had reached a place of safety. This was the principal reason why he made his entry into the city on horseback.

The 15th of October, which had been universally expected to give birth to important events, was now quietly passed. For many weeks the city had not been so tranquil as it was on the night of that day. Nothing but the incessant *Qui vive?* at the gates, denoted the presence of the troops. On my return about eight o'clock from the suburbs, I was suddenly surprised by an unusual phenomenon: in the direction of Pegau, I saw three white rockets ascend to a great height amid the darkness. I stood still, and waited to observe what would follow. In about a minute four red ones rose above the horizon, apparently from Halle. After this there was nothing more to be seen. That they were signals could not be doubted, any more than that those signals must have been made by the combined troops.

I concluded that they must have armies in those quarters, and that they were informing one another by these luminous messengers of the points at which they had arrived. It now became more certain than ever that the 16th would be the great day that should decide the fate of Germany. I expressed my conjectures to several French officers, that, according to all appearance, fresh armies of the allies were on their march toward Leipzig. They contradicted me point-blank; partly because, as they said, the Crown-Prince of Sweden and General Blücher had been obliged to retreat precipitately across the Elbe, as an immense French army was in full march upon Berlin; and partly because they were convinced that the reinforcements which might be coming up could be of no great consequence; and were confident, that, at all events, they should be perfectly prepared to receive the enemy. Never did they make so sure of the most complete victory as they did previously to the then approaching engagement. Besides the French in garrison in the city, there were many German troops, who expressed little hope, and, on the other hand, declared their resolution to make no resistance, but to pass over to the allies, as many of their comrades had already done; and there was no reason to doubt their sincerity.

Thus passed the second day, between hope and fear.

A Day of Battle
16th October

The dawn of the 16th of October was enveloped in a thick fog. It was gloomy, rainy, and cold. It was imagined that the hostile armies, though so eager for the combat, would restrain their ardour to engage till the fog should have cleared away. Soon after six, however, the thunder of the artillery began to roll from Liebertwolkwitz. It grew more violent, and approached nearer;—this was probably the moment when the Austrians stormed that place. The firing *en pelotons* was already heard. From our elevated position we could discern nothing, the dense fog concealing every object at the distance of one hundred paces. About ten, the artillery thundered along the whole line of battle. The atmosphere became clearer, and the clouds dispersed. Every flash from the cannon was distinctly visible on the side of Konnewitz. Already a thousand engines of death hurled destruction among the contending armies. The fire of *jägers* and sharp-shooters rattled on all sides, and we soon discovered whole ranges of battalions and regiments. It was a general engagement;—that was evident enough to everyone, even though he had never before heard a cannon fired in all his life. On the side of the Halle and Ranstädt gates all was yet quiet, and I began to imagine that my rockets had deceived me. For six hours the guns had roared, and all the lines were enveloped in clouds of smoke, through which the flashes incessantly darted like lightning. As yet neither party seemed to have receded an inch. The thunders of the artillery still continued to proceed from the same spot. No longer could the firing of single guns be distinguished; hundreds were every moment discharged, and united in one single protracted roar. How many victims must already have strewed the field!

At length, about eleven o'clock, a considerable change seemed to have taken place. The firing did not appear more distant, but became less general; single shots were heard, and the combatants seemed disposed to make a pause in the work of death. All on a sudden a new and tremendous cannonade commenced beyond Lindenau, towards Lützen, not much more than half a league from the city. The batteries of the allies seemed to fire from Kleinschocher: those of the French were posted on the heights of Lindenau. The corps of Count Giulay had arrived there, and now it appeared that my interpretation of the rockets was correct.

I then turned my eyes quickly towards the north, in the direction of Halle, where before there was little or nothing to be seen. How was I astonished when I now beheld lines of soldiers stretching farther than the eye could reach, and fresh columns advancing behind them. It appeared as if the troops which had been so furiously engaged the whole morning were but the advanced guards of the immense armies that now extended themselves more and more before me.

Whence the French lines which were so rapidly ranged opposite to them could have sprung, I am yet at a loss to conceive: an hour before, I should have estimated them at scarcely 10,000 men; and, what I now saw, my inexperienced eye computed at more than 200,000 on both sides.

This prodigious army seemed about to form in order of battle. A few cannon-shot which it fired were probably designed only to announce its arrival to the other chiefs. Immediately afterwards, the cannonade beyond Lindenau, which had lasted about two hours, entirely ceased. On the left wing of the French the action was still very vigorously continued. It was about twelve o'clock when we descended, to learn what accounts had meanwhile been received in the city, that our relations with the lower world might not be totally suspended.

Before the residence of our sovereign there was a crowd of officers of all ranks. The city-guard was drawn out on parade as well as the grenadier-guard. A full band was playing, by French order, though nobody could conceive what was the meaning of all this, while the cannon were yet thundering before the city. We soon learned that the allies had sustained a total defeat; that an Austrian prince, the Archduke Ferdinand, had lost an arm, and been taken prisoner with 40,000 men; and that an immense quantity of artillery had been captured. This intelligence had been forwarded by Marshal Ney from the field of battle, and preparations were instantly made to celebrate the victory. A regiment of the French guards marched to the promenade before the city—now, alas! an offensive sewer,—and, agreeably to command, expressed their exultation in the acquisition of these new laurels by a loud *Vive l'empereur!*

Of the citizens, but a very small portion took part in their joy; for what else could they have expected from such a victory than inevitable death by famine? The more intelligent shook their heads; and in truth there were but too many reasons to suspect the truth of the account. If you asked the wounded, who in troops either hobbled or were carried in at the gates, the answer, was, *Les Cosaques ont encore la même position*—(The Cossacks are still in the same position). None of them had heard anything about captured cannon, but they well knew that they had themselves lost five pieces that morning. I was unable to comprehend how the French commander-in-chief, possessing in so eminent a degree the quality of a correct military *coup d'oeil*, could so early announce that he had won the battle, when such numerous armies of the allies had but just arrived upon the field, and had not yet fired a single shot. Country-people, who had fled from the neighbourhood of Grimma, declared that a fresh army of Russians, under general Bennigsen, was in full march towards that place. In truth, only a small part of the allied forces had yet been engaged. Bennigsen, the Crown-Prince of Sweden, and Field-Marshal Blücher, had not yet entered the lists. If this fiction was intended merely to pacify our king at the expense of truth, it was evident that this object could not be attained without compromising him;—a kind of treatment wholly unmerited by a prince who was never guilty of wilful falsehood.[4]

In the midst of these rejoicings for the victory, the thunder of the artillery was again heard from Lindenau. The tremendous roar was almost immediately repeated from Taucha, Wiederitsch, and Breitenfeld. The Swedish army

---

4. The following fact will serve to show how completely the King of Saxony was duped by the imperial plunderer:—The king was standing with one of his ministers at a window of his palace in Dresden at the moment when a drove of remarkably fine cattle, intended for the French army, passed by. His majesty took occasion to praise the paternal care which the emperor manifested for his troops, in procuring them such abundant supplies of provisions. "But," replied the minister, "your majesty is surely not aware that it is at the expense of your poor subjects, as Napoleon pays for nothing."—"Impossible!" exclaimed the king with evident indignation. While they were yet in conversation, intelligence was brought from his domain of Pillnitz, which is well known to be the most beautiful in Saxony, that the French had taken away by force all his fine cattle, and just driven them through the city. These were the very same beasts which he had seen passing, and now for the first time he became sensible at what price Bonaparte obtained provisions from his faithful ally.

and that of Blücher were now engaged. We again repaired to our lofty station. There was not a point round the city where the fatal engines were not dealing forth destruction. We knew not which way first to direct the glass.

"Only look here," cried one.

"Oh! that's nothing at all," replied another, "you must come this way."

"You none of you see anything," exclaimed a third: "you must look yonder—there the cavalry are cutting away—and hark how the fresh artillery is beginning to fire."

It was singular enough that just at the very point where the allies were reported to have sustained so signal a defeat, that is to say, on their left wing, at Liebertwolkwitz, the cannonade again became the most violent. Fresh troops, with artillery, including a large body of Polish cavalry, were seen hastening out by the Ranstädt gate towards Lindenau. Napoleon himself rode with the King of Naples along the causeway to the Kuhthurm (cow-tower), as it is called, probably to observe how things were going on.

The allies strove to make themselves masters of the pass near Lindenau. Their infantry had actually penetrated into the village, but was driven back, and this was succeeded by a tremendous fire of riflemen, which was near enough for us to distinguish the discharge of every single piece. I remarked on this occasion the incredible exertions of the French *voltigeurs*, who defended a ditch near the Kuhthurm, ran to and fro on the bank with inconceivable agility, availed themselves of the protection afforded by every tree and every hedge, and fired away as briskly as though they had carried with them the Confederation of the Rhine, as their own property, in their cartouche boxes. Cannon-balls and shells had fallen in the village itself, which was set on fire in several places.

Whether friend or enemy had the advantage it was impossible to judge, on account of the broken nature of the ground and the woods, behind which the engagement was the hottest It was evident that one party exerted itself as strenuously to defend as the other did to take this important position. The French retained it; therefore the prize of victory in this instance must be adjudged to them. At Breitenfeld, Lindenthal, and Wiederitsch, the fortune of the day was different. There the lines of the allies evidently advanced. The cannonade was an infallible barometer. The French artillery receded, and was already driven back so close upon Gohlis and Eutritzsch, that the balls of their opponents fell in both villages.

Night drew on: the vast field of battle became gradually enveloped in darkness, and the horizon was now illumined by the flashes of the guns alone, followed at long intervals by the low thunder of the report. The battle had lasted the whole day all round the city. The church-clocks struck six; and, as if all parties had unanimously agreed to suspend at this moment the horrid work of slaughter, the last cannon-shot was fired beyond Lindenau. The fire of small arms, however, was yet kept up; but, as though the mortal struggle became more and more faint, that too gradually ceased. Nothing now was seen around the horizon but one immense circle of many thousand watch-fires. In all directions appeared blazing villages, and from their number might be inferred the havoc occasioned by this arduous day. Its effects were still more plainly manifested when we descended into the streets.

Thousands of wounded had poured in at all the gates, and every moment increased their numbers. Many had lost an arm or a leg, and yet limped along with pitiable moans. As for a dressing for their wounds, that was a thing which could not yet be thought of; the poor wretches had themselves bound them up with some old rag or other as well as they were able. All of them were seeking hospitals, the arrangements for which had, in truth, been most miserably neglected by the French. Upon the whole, I have had occasion to remark that the soldier, who has been crippled in the service, and incapacitated for further warfare, has nowhere so little regard paid to his situation as in the French army. At least such is the case just at the moment when he has most need of attention, that is to say, just after he is wounded. No carriages or other conveyances were provided for the removal of these mangled and mutilated soldiers, though the lives of thousands might perhaps have been preserved by such a precaution.

When the combined Russian and Prussian army marched six months before to Lützen, and prepared for battle, the amplest provision was made in regard to this point; and it is well known that their army was thus enabled to carry off by far the greater part of the wounded, and to afford them medical relief. Such, on the contrary, were the arrangements of the French, that, five days after that engagement, soldiers with their wounds still undressed, and near perishing for want of sustenance, were found on the field of battle, and at last owed their preservation chiefly to the surgeons and inhabitants of this city. To each French column are attached a great number of *ambulances*, but they are never to be found where they are most wanted. It is universally asserted that the French army surgeons are very skilful men; but, as they seem to consult their own convenience in a very high degree, and their number is too small—for a complete regiment has but five—the arrangements for hospitals in a campaign during which several great battles take place, and in which it is found necessary to crowd the sick and wounded much too closely together, as was the case in Saxony, are always most deplorable. But to return from this digression:

For the reception of the wounded, in this instance, orders

had been given to clear out the corn-magazine, which is capable of accommodating about 2,500. Each of these poor fellows received a written ticket at the outer gate of the city, and was directed to that hospital. The persons who superintended this business never gave it a thought to distribute only such a number of these billets as the building would hold of sick, but continued to send all that came to the corn-magazine, long after it was too full to admit another individual. Overjoyed on having at last found the spot, the wretched cripple exerted his last remains of strength, that he might obtain relief as speedily as possible at the hands of the surgeons. Judge then of the feelings of the unfortunate man when his hopes were here most cruelly disappointed; when he found many hundreds of his fellow-sufferers moaning with anguish on the wet stones, without straw to lie upon, without shelter of any kind, without medical or surgical attendance, nay, even without a drop of water, for which they so often and so earnestly petitioned;—when he was peremptorily refused admittance at the door, and he too had no other resource than to seek a couch like the rest upon the hard pavement, which his wounds very often were unable to endure. No more attention was here paid to him than the stones on which he gave vent to his anguish. Many hobbled farther in quest of something to appease the cravings of hunger and thirst. But who could give it them? Extreme want had long prevailed in the city; the very inhabitants had great trouble and difficulty to obtain for money sufficient to make a scanty meal for themselves and their families. The fainting soldier might think himself fortunate if his solicitations procured him a crust of bread or an apple. Thousands were not so lucky.

Such was the state of things at the magazine; such was the spectacle exhibited in all the streets, and especially in the market-place, where every corner provided with a shelter was converted into an hospital. The consequences were inevitable. Many; as might naturally be expected, perished, in the night, of hunger, agony, and cold. Their lot was enviable—they no longer needed any human assistance. What heart would not have bled at such scenes of horror!—and yet it was the very countrymen of these unfortunate wretches who seemed to care the least about them, and passed by with the most frigid indifference, probably because they are so familiarized with such spectacles. O ye mothers, ye fathers, ye sisters of France, had ye here beheld your agonized sons and brothers, the sight, like a hideous phantom, would surely have haunted you to the last moment of your lives. The laurels acquired by your nation have indeed been purchased at a most exorbitant price.

I have forgotten to mention a circumstance worthy of notice in the history of this day. It is this; that in the midst of the cannonade all round Leipzig—when the whole city shook with the thunders of the artillery, and the general engagement had, strictly speaking, but just commenced—all the bells of the churches were rung by French command, to celebrate the victory won in the forenoon. Such an instance was certainly never afforded by any battle which had scarcely begun, and terminated in the total and decisive overthrow of him who had already fancied himself mounted in triumph upon the car of victory. This day, however, the engagement still remained undecided, according to the reports of those who returned from different points of the field of battle. The French had stood as if rooted to the spot—the allies, like rocks of granite. The former had fought like men, the latter like lions. Both parties, inspired with mutual respect, desisted from hostilities during the night.

The combined troops, who had not been able in two sanguinary days to bring the contest to an issue, had, however, during that time gained several essential advantages.

They had ascertained the strength of their antagonist, and made themselves acquainted with the nature of the ground. They knew what points were the most vulnerable, and could thence infer how the enemy would manoeuvre. They were enabled to make their own dispositions accordingly, and to give to the plan of the grand engagement that perfection by which it is so peculiarly characterized. In this point of view the allies had, without our suspecting it, advanced a considerable step on the night of the third day.

The Truce

17th October

According to the general opinion of the inhabitants of Leipzig, the 17th was destined to be the important day on which the last act of the great tragedy was to be performed. We were, however, mistaken. The morning came, and we heard nothing from either side. We had long ceased to take notice of single shots. The French lines occupied Probstheide, and all the points where they had the preceding day been posted. The order of battle had, however, been considerably changed. The vast armies which had been drawn up to the west and north had almost entirely disappeared. In the forenoon a cannonade commenced about Gohlis, but soon ceased again. In the meadows between the city and Lindenau were posted some cavalry. At a greater distance but few troops were to be seen; and the allies seemed to have renounced any farther attempts on that pass.

The left wing of the French grand army extended to Abtnaundorf, and had strong corps posted as far as Taucha; the centre stretched behind the Kohlgärten and Stötteritz to Probstheide, and the right wing reached beyond Konnewitz to the wood and the Elster. Several lines were advanced to Markleeberg. The combined army occupied parallel positions. You will not expect me to say more respecting the order of battle, especially as a circumstantial account of it has already appeared.

The motives which occasioned a kind of truce to be observed during the whole of this day are unknown to me. This phenomenon was, the more surprising, as Napoleon is not accustomed long to defer business of such importance. From what I can learn, there was no parleying, as has been asserted, between the contending parties. Several Frenchmen assigned, as a reason, that the emperor expected a strong reinforcement of three corps, and therefore undertook nothing on this day. On all sides columns of smoke were yet seen rising from the villages that were reduced to ashes. All at once the church of Probstheide also appeared in flames. It soon fell in, and is now totally demolished. This fire is said to have been occasioned by negligence.

All the large edifices in the city were now selected for the purpose of being converted into hospitals. The number of the wounded kept continually augmenting, and by far the greatest part of them had still no other shelter than the streets. Many, though after three days of suffering, were yet unable to obtain any assistance. The king resolutely remained in the city, in order, as the event showed, there to await his fate, whatever it might be. Our condition became every moment more alarming; and, in proportion as our anxiety grew more painful, our hopes diminished. What will become of us before this time tomorrow? Was the general question on the evening of that day, and we looked forward with dejection and despondency to the morrow's dawn. We felt much less anxiety in the midst of the thunder of the artillery than we did at the close of this fourth day. It resembled the dead calm which precedes the impending storm. The combined troops took their leave of us for the night, as they had done on the preceding, with the discharge of three cannon. It had been Sunday, and you might almost have imagined that the contending parties had suffered it to pass thus peaceably, out of respect to the commandment—*Thou shalt keep the sabbath-day holy.*

A Day of Decision
18th October

The 18th of October at length appeared. It was a day equal in importance to many a century; and the fewer History can produce that deserve to be classed along with it, the more memorable it will remain. All that preceded it had merely opened the way, and there were yet almost inaccessible cliffs to climb before we could flatter ourselves with the hope of reaching the wished-for goal. The leaders of the allies had already shown the ablest French generals, in several grand engagements, that they possessed sufficient means and talents to dissolve the charm of their invincibility. They were now about to enter the lists with the hero whom a thousand panegyrists, during a period of near twenty years, had extolled far above the greatest generals of ancient and modern times; whose enemies had to boast of but one victory over him at most—a victory which he himself did not admit, as he ascribed the total destruction of his army in Russia to physical causes alone. It was the conqueror of Marengo, Austerlitz, Friedland, Ratisbon, Wagram, and Mojaisk. Fresh laurels entwined his brow at Lützen, Bautzen, and Dresden. Here at Leipzig the allies attempted to wrest them from him who grasps so firmly. It was easy to foresee that with unshaken resolution he would risk all, in order, as on former occasions, to gain all, and to put an end to the campaign with a single blow. He seemed to contemplate nothing less than the utter annihilation of the allies, as all the bridges far and near were broken down to cut off their retreat. Whether the situation in which he had placed himself was such as to justify these hopes, I shall leave to the decision of those who are better qualified to judge. His confidence in victory must, however, have been very strong, as he had made such inadequate preparations for his own retreat.

The action commenced in the centre of the French army beyond Probstheide, probably with the storming of the villages in its front, for we afterwards learned that they were several times taken and recovered. They have been more or less reduced to heaps of rubbish. That the work of slaughter might be completed on this day, it had been begun with the first dawn of morning. So early as nine o'clock all the immense lines from Taucha to Konnewitz were engaged. As the latter village lay nearest to us, we could see what was passing there the most distinctly. From Lösnig, a village situated beyond Konnewitz, a hollow, about two thousand paces in length, runs from north-west to south-east. It is bordered with a narrow skirt of wood, consisting of alders, limes, and oaks, and forms an angle with the village. Beyond this line were advanced several French batteries, the incessant movements of which, as well as every single shot, might be clearly distinguished with our glasses.

To make myself better acquainted with this neighbourhood, I explored two days afterwards this part of the field of battle, and found that the French artillery must there have formed an open triangle; for the road which runs straight from Leipzig, behind Konnewitz through Dehlis and Lösnig, of course from north to south, was also lined by French batteries. The houses of those villages had served them for a *point d'appui* in the rear, and were most of them dread-

fully shattered by the balls of the Austrians. The artillery of
the latter seems to have had a great advantage in regard to
the ground. The French cannon brought into the line from
Konnewitz to Dehlis and Lösnig stood in a hollow—those
of the Austrians on eminences. These last had moreover the
advantage of enfilading the two angles formed by the batteries of the French. That this had actually been the case
was evident from the numbers of French cannoniers and
horses lying dead in rows in the line of the above-men-
tioned villages, where they had been swept down by the
guns of their opponents.

On the eminences where the hostile cannon were
planted the number of dead was much smaller, and these
were apparently not artillery-men, but infantry, who were
probably engaged in covering those batteries. The firearms
which lay beside them confirmed the conjecture. This pass
must nevertheless have been obstinately defended, as it was
not taken the whole day. The fire of musketry grew more
and more brisk—a proof that the combatants were already
in close action. The French *tirailleurs* could not be driven
out of the woods, on which their right wing was supported. We remarked frequent charges of cavalry, which seemed
to decide nothing. All the villages lying beyond Konnewitz,
on the road to Borna, as far as Markleeberg, were on fire.

The thunder from the French centre, as well as from the
left wing, gradually approached nearer to the city. The sev-
enth corps, under General Reynier, was in the left wing,
and posted towards Taucha. It was principally composed of
Saxons. They had just come into action, and the allies had
already brought up a great number of guns against them. To
the no small astonishment and consternation of their leader,
they suddenly shouldered their arms, marched forward in
close files with their artillery, and went over to the enemy.

Several French battalions, misled by this movement,

joined them, and were immediately disarmed and made prisoners by the allies. The French cuirassiers, suspecting the design of the Saxons, followed, apparently with the intention of falling upon them. The Saxons faced about, and compelled them, by a smart fire of musketry, to return. A volley of small arms was discharged after them, but with no more effect—it did them no injury. Their horse-artillery turned about, and soon dismounted that of the French. They were greeted with a joyful *hurrah!* by the Cossacks, who cordially shook hands with their new comrades. The Saxons desired to be immediately led back to the attack of the French.

The hearts of these soldiers individually had long glowed with revenge for all the devastations committed in their native land by their allies and companions in arms, for whom they had so often shed their blood in torrents. The generals of the allies refused on very good grounds to comply with their desire. The Saxons marched a league into the rear of the field of battle, and there bivouacked. Their artillery only was afterwards invited to take part in the engagement, and did great execution. This circumstance had an essential influence on the issue of the contest, inasmuch as the defection of a body of more than 8000 men facilitated the advance of the right wing of the allies. But for this step the Saxons would have fared very badly, as their opponents had already ranged upwards of thirty pieces of cannon against their line, and were bringing up still more to the attack. These now proved the more galling to the ranks of the French, who were driven back almost to the Kohlgärten.

From my position this advance of the allies was not to be perceived except by the approach of the thunder of the artillery. The French centre yet stood immoveable; at least we could not observe from the city any change which denoted a retrograde movement. The sanguinary character of this tremendous conflict might be inferred from the thousands of wounded, who hobbled, crawled, and were carried in at the gates. Among the latter were many officers of rank. If you inquired of those who returned from the field, how the battle was going on, the reply almost invariably was—"Badly enough,—the enemy is very strong."

A Saxon cuirassier declared, without reserve, that it might be considered as decided, adding, "We have lost a deal of ground already."

Stötteritz and Schönefeld were stormed the same evening. All the streets were covered with wounded, and fortunate were they who could find a shelter. As for surgical aid and refreshments, these were not to be thought of. A far greater number of those miserable wretches were yet left behind in the villages, as might be seen from the detached limbs, which were piled in heaps, especially at Probstheide.

Had any of the allied corps succeeded this day in penetrating on any side into our city, nothing less than the total destruction of the French army would probably have been the consequence; since it might from this place, as from the centre of the field of battle, have fallen upon the rear of any part of the French force, and have hemmed in both the centre and the wings. This misfortune Napoleon had taken good care to prevent. He now felt, however, that his strength was broken, and that he was no longer in a condition to maintain the contest. He resolved upon retreat, but carefully sought to conceal this intention from his enemies.

Though night had come on; yet the cannon thundered as furiously as in the morning, and the fire of musketry was brisker than ever. A long column, with an endless train of artillery, was seen defiling from Probstheide to Konnewitz. Again I trembled for the cause of the allies. These, I imagined, were the French guards, marching to the attack of the right wing. Now methought the moment had arrived when Napoleon would strike the decisive blow, which he had so often deferred till the very last hour. Soon afterwards the cannonade seemed to gain redoubled vigour, and continued an hour without intermission, so that every house in the city was shaken. As, however, it at length ceased without removing to a greater distance, we naturally concluded that this last attack had proved unsuccessful. More than ten great conflagrations illumined the whole horizon amid the obscurity of night.

The excessive bustle in the city rendered it impossible for us to observe that the retreat had in fact commenced. The greatest part of the persons attached to the army had already left the city, while the others were making all the requisite preparations for their departure. Most of them had wonderfully changed the tone in which they had spoken the preceding day. They now talked of the miseries of war, deplored the sufferings of the people, and declared that peace would be the greatest of blessings for all parties.

The multitude of French officers here was so great, that even those of high rank on the staff were obliged to put up with the most wretched accommodations, for which they paid handsomely, leaving their horses and equipages in the street, where the former frequently ran away. One of these officers sought a night's lodging in a mean house in the author's neighbourhood. He was called up at midnight, and informed that his column had just begun to retreat. He inquired whether the whole army was doing the same—the messenger replied that he did not know. This circumstance first confirmed my belief that the French had sustained a defeat, and rendered the conjecture that their whole army was retreating highly probable. Many French *employés* and soldiers had, several days before, while they yet had an opportunity, exchanged their uniform for the plainest attire, that, under this peaceful *ægis*, they might the more calmly await the issue of events; and that, in case the allies should come upon them too unexpectedly, they might, under the disguise of honest citizens, hasten away to their beloved Rhine without being challenged by the lances of the Cossacks. With greater composure than any of them did General Bertrand, the governor of the city, who, perhaps, as an intelligent officer, was the least confident of victory, look forward to the event. He abandoned not his post at the precipitate departure of the emperor, and was in consequence made prisoner the following day.

Such was the conclusion of the fifth day. It beheld a field of battle, of unparalleled extent, strewed with slain; and left one of the most flourishing districts of Saxony, as it were, one general conflagration. With anxious solicitude the people of Leipzig awaited its coming, and with expectations unfulfilled they witnessed its close. Though it appeared probable to us all, that, in this colossal engagement, victory had wholly forsaken the Gallic eagles, still the fate of our city was far from being decided. We were yet in the midst of the crater of the tremendous volcano, which by one mighty effort might hurl us into atoms, and leave behind scarcely a vestige of our existence. Napoleon had received a severe blow; and now it behoved him to oppose an immediate barrier to the impetuous course of the conquerors, and to prevent the total loss of his yet remaining army, artillery, and baggage. The only bulwark that he could employ for this purpose was Leipzig. All that art had formerly done to render it a defensive position had long since disappeared. Planks, hedges, and mud walls, were scarcely calculated to resist the butt-end of a musket. This deficiency it was everywhere necessary to supply by living walls, and that was in fact done in such a way as filled us all with consternation.

The Allies Victorious
19th October

At day-break on the 19th the allies put the finishing
hand to the great work. A considerable part of the French
army, with an immense quantity of artillery, had already
passed through and into the city with great precipitation.
The troops that covered the retreat were furiously attacked,
and driven on all sides into the city. Napoleon attempted
to arrest the progress of victory by an expedient which had
so often before produced an extraordinary effect, that is,
by negotiation. A proposal was made to evacuate the city
voluntarily, and to declare the Saxon troops there as neu-
tral, on condition that the retreating army should have sufficient time allowed to withdraw from it with its artillery
and wagon-train, and to reach a certain specified point.

The allies too clearly perceived what an important advantage would in this case be gained by the French army,
which was less anxious for the fate of the city than to effect its own escape. These terms were rejected, and several hundred pieces of artillery began to play upon Leipzig.
Our fate would have been decided had the allied sovereigns
cherished sentiments less generous and humane than they
did. It behoved them to gain possession of Leipzig at any
rate; and this object they might have accomplished in the

shortest way, and with inconsiderable loss to themselves, if they had bombarded it for one single hour with shells, red-hot balls, and Congreve rockets, with which an English battery that accompanied them was provided.

Their philanthropic spirits, on the contrary, revolted at the idea of involving the innocent population of a German city in the fate of Moscow and Saragossa. They resolved to storm the town, and to support the troops employed in this duty with artillery no farther than was necessary to silence the enemy, and to force their way through the palisaded avenues and gates. Meanwhile the discharges of artillery, quite close to us, were so tremendous, that each seemed sufficient to annihilate the city. The King of Saxony himself sent flags of truce, entreating that it might be spared. The allies replied that this should be done in as far as the defence of the enemy might render it practicable: they promised, moreover, security to persons and property after the place should be taken, and to enforce as rigid discipline as it was possible on such an occasion. To these assurances they annexed the condition that no French should be secreted in the city, declaring that every house in which one or more of them should be found would run the risk of being reduced to ashes.

The cannon, though only in a proportionally small number from the north and east, immediately began to play. They were partly directed against the palisades at the gates, partly against the French artillery which defended the avenues. For more than two hours balls and shells from the east and north frequently fell in the city itself, and in the suburbs. Many a time I was filled with astonishment at the effects of one single ball, which often penetrated through two thick walls, and pursued its course still farther. Though they seldom fell in the streets, it was impossible to venture abroad without imminent hazard of life, as these tremendous visitors beat down large fragments of roofs, chimneys, and walls, which, tumbling with a frightful crash, threatened to bury every passenger beneath their ruins.

Still greater havoc was made by the shells, which, bursting as soon as they had descended, immediately set their new habitations in flames. Fortunately for us, but few of these guests were sent into the city. The most that fell came from the north, that is, in the direction of Halle. Three times did fires break out in the Brühl, which, in a short consumed several back buildings contiguous to the city wall, and nothing but the instantaneous measures adopted for their extinction prevented farther damage. The allies had no other object, in dispatching these ministers of destruction, than to show the retreating enemy, who, in the general confusion and bustle, could no longer move either forward or backward, that, if they now forbore to annihilate him, it was because the innocent citizens might be involved in equal destruction with the fugitives. Pfaffendorf, a farm-house near the north side of the city, had previously been set on fire, when the Russian *jägers* had penetrated thither through the Rosenthal, and was consumed to the very walls. As this place had been converted into an hospital, many poor fellows there fell a sacrifice to the flames.

You may easily conceive the sensations of the inhabitants of the upper town when we beheld the black clouds of smoke rising from the lower, while the incessant fire of the artillery rendered it impossible for us to repair thither, to obtain information or to afford assistance. Here, as everywhere else, the fears of the inhabitants were wound up to the highest pitch. A cry was raised that several streets were already in flames, and every one now hastened to his own house, that he might be at hand in case a similar accident should happen there. It became more and more dangerous to remain in the upper stories, which the inhabitants accordingly quitted, and betook themselves to the kitchens and cellars. If such were the terrors of the inmates, old and young, the fears and anxiety of the French who chanced to be in the houses surpassed all description. Many of them were seen weeping like children, and starting convulsively at every report of the cannon. In the midst of this hideous uproar I made another attempt to learn what was passing in the suburbs. In the streets I found inexpressible confusion, people running in all directions, officers driving their men to the gates.

Cries and shouts resounded from all quarters, though very few of the persons from whom they proceeded knew what they would be at. At this time cartouche boxes and muskets were to be seen thrown away here and there in the streets. The Saxon grenadier guards were drawn out with wonderful composure and grounded arms, before the royal residence. Every unarmed person anxiously sought to gain the nearest house, but commonly found it shut against him. Several had already lost their lives or been severely wounded by the balls which fell in all directions. Napoleon was still in the city; he was at this moment with our king, with whom he had an animated conversation, which lasted near an hour. Soon afterwards I saw him, accompanied by the King of Naples, proceeding on horseback toward the Ranstädt gate. I had meanwhile taken the opportunity of slipping into a house which overlooks that street, and now for the first time beheld a French retreat in the height of its confusion. Not a vestige of regularity was any where observable.

The horse and foot guards poured along in mingled disorder. They would probably have marched in quicker time, had they been permitted by the wagons and cannon, which were locked in one another, and obstructed the way. Between these they were obliged to pass singly, and I really thought that it would be at least six hours before they could all have effected their passage. Immense droves of cattle were cooped up among the crowd. These seemed to be objects of particular concern to the French. They sought out a space, however narrow, along the town-ditch, by which they might drive forward their horned favourites.

Whoever was bold enough, and had any hopes of being able to conduct these animals into his own habitation, had now an opportunity of making an advantageous bargain. A few pieces of silver might be carried off with much greater facility than a huge clumsy ox. Notwithstanding all the efforts to preserve this valuable booty from the general wreck, it was absolutely impossible to save the whole of it. Many horned cattle and horses were left behind, and now innocently sought a scanty repast by the city-walls. That, amidst all this "confusion worse confounded," there was no want of shouting and blustering, you may easily imagine, though nobody got forward any faster for all this noise.

On a sudden we saw at a distance the emperor himself, with not a numerous retinue, advancing on horseback into the midst of this chaos. He got through better than I expected. I afterwards learned that he took a by-road through a garden to the outer Ranstädt gate. Prince Poniatowsky attempted, higher up, to ford the Elster. The banks on each side are of considerable height, soft and swampy; the current itself narrow, but in this part uncommonly deep and muddy. How so expert a rider should have lost the management of his horse, I cannot imagine. According to report, the animal plunged headlong into the water with him, so that he could not possibly recover himself. He fell a victim to his temerity, and was drowned. His body was found several days afterwards, and interred with all the military honours due to his rank.[5]

---

5. Prince Joseph Poniatowsky was nephew to Stanislaus Augustus, the last king of Poland, and there is no doubt that he was cajoled into a subservience to the views of the French emperor by the flattering prospect of the restoration of his country to its former rank (continued opposite)

As the commander-in-chief had so precipitately quitted the city, we could no longer doubt the proximity of the enemy to our walls. The fire of the artillery and musketry in the place, which gradually approached nearer, was a much more convincing proof of this than we desired. The men already began to cut away the traces, in order to save the horses. The bustle among the soldiers augmented; a weak rearguard had taken post in Reichel's garden, to keep the allies in check, in case they should penetrate into the high road.

We thought them still at a considerable distance, when a confused cry suddenly proclaimed that the Russians had

---

among the nations of Europe. The circumstances attending his death, as related by his aid-de-camp, are as follow:—On the 19th of October, when the French army began to retreat, the prince was charged by Napoleon with the defence of that part of the suburbs of Leipzig which lies nearest to the Borna road. For this service he had only 2000 Polish infantry assigned him. Perceiving the French columns on his left flank in full retreat, and the bridge completely choked up with their artillery and carriages, so that there was no possibility of getting over it, he drew his sabre, and, turning to the officers who were about him, "Gentlemen," said he, "it is better to fall with honour." With these words he rushed, at the head of a few Polish cuirassiers and the officers surrounding him, upon the advancing columns of the allies. He had been previously wounded on the 14th and 16th, and on this occasion also received a musket-ball in his left arm. He nevertheless pushed forward, but found the suburbs full of the allied troops, who hastened up to take him prisoner. He cut his way through them, received another wound through his cross, threw himself into the Pleisse, and with the assistance of his officers reached the opposite bank in safety, leaving his horse behind in the river. Though much exhausted he mounted another, and proceeded to the Elster, which was already lined by Saxon and Prussian riflemen. Seeing them coming upon him on all sides, he plunged into the river, and instantly sunk, together with his horse. Several officers, who threw themselves in after him, were likewise drowned; and others were taken on the bank or in the water. The body of the prince was found on the fifth day (Oct. 24), and taken out of the water by a fisherman. He was dressed in his gala uniform, the epaulets of which were studded with diamonds. His fingers were covered with rings set with brilliants; and his pockets contained snuff-boxes of great value and other trinkets. Many of those articles were eagerly purchased by the Polish officers who were made prisoners, evidently for the purpose of being transmitted to his family; so that the whole produced the fisherman a very considerable sum.

stormed the outer Peter's gate, and were coming round from the Rossplatz. The French were evidently alarmed. The Russian *jägers* came upon them all at once, at full speed, with tremendous huzzas and fixed bayonets, and discharged their pieces singly, without stopping. I now thought it advisable to quit my dangerous post, and hasten home with all possible expedition. I was informed by the way that the Prussians had that moment stormed the Grimma gate, and would be in the city in a few minutes.

On all sides was heard the firing of small arms, intermixed at times with the reports of the artillery, already playing upon the wagon-train in the suburbs. Musket-balls, passing over the city wall, likewise whizzed through the streets; and, when I ventured to put my head out of the window, I observed with horror, not far from my house, two Prussian *jägers* pursuing and firing at some Frenchmen who were running away. Behind them I heard the storm-march, and huzzas and shouts of *Long live Frederic William!* from thousands of voices. A company of Baden *jägers* was charged with the defence of the inner Peter's gate. These troops immediately abandoned their post, and ran as fast as their legs would carry them to the market-place, where they halted, and, like the Saxon grenadier guards, fired not a single shot.

Thus the so long feared and yet wished-for hour was at length arrived. What we should never have expected after the 2nd of May, namely, to see a single Prussian again at Leipzig, was nevertheless come to pass. They had then left us as friends, and, by their exemplary conduct, had acquired our highest respect. We bore them, as well as the Russians, in the most honourable remembrance. They now appeared as enemies, whose duty had imposed on them the task of storming the city. Our sons and brothers had fought against them. What might not be our fate? We had not forgotten that which befell Lübeck, seven years before, under similar circumstances. But they were the warriors of Alexander, Francis, Frederic William, and Charles John; terrible as destroying angels to the foe, kind and generous to the defenceless citizen.

As far as the author's knowledge extends, not a man was guilty of the smallest excess within our walls. They even paid in specie for bread, tobacco, and brandy. The suburbs, indeed, fared not quite so well. There many an inhabitant suffered severely; but how was it possible for the commanders to be present everywhere, and to prevent all irregularities, after a conflict which had raged in every corner of the city? Would you compare the victors, upon the whole, with our late friends and protectors, go through all Saxony, and then judge in whose favour the parallel must be drawn.

It was half past one o'clock when the allies penetrated into the city. The artillery had been but little used on this occasion, and in the interior of the place not at all. Had not the allies shown so much tenderness for the town, they might have spared the sacrifice of some hundreds of their brave soldiers. They employed infantry in the assault, that the city might not be utterly destroyed. The grand work was now nearly accomplished. Obstinately as the French in general defended themselves, they were, nevertheless, unable to withstand the iron masses of their assailants. They were overthrown in all quarters, and driven out of the place.

Aftermath

The streets, especially in the suburbs, were strewed with dead. The writer often counted eight in a very small space. In about an hour you might venture abroad without danger in all parts of the town. But what sights now met the eye! Leipzig, including the suburbs, cannot occupy an area of much less than one (German) square mile. In this extent there was scarcely a spot not covered with houses but bore evidence of the sanguinary conflict. The ground was covered with carcasses, and the horses were particularly numerous. The nearer you approached to the Ranstädt gate, the thicker lay the dead bodies. The Ranstädt causeway, which is crossed by what is called the Mühlgraben (milldam), exhibited a spectacle peculiarly horrid. Men and horses were everywhere to be seen; driven into the water, they had found their grave in it, and projected in hideous groups above its surface. Here the storming columns from all the gates, guided by the fleeing foe, had for the most part united, and had found a sure mark for every shot in the closely crowded masses of the enemy.

But the most dreadful sight of all was that which presented itself in the beautiful Richter's garden, once the ornament of the city, on that side where it joins the Elster. There the cavalry must have been engaged; at least I there saw a great number of French cuirasses lying about. All along the bank, heads, arms, and feet, appeared above the water. Numbers, in attempting to ford the treacherous river, had here perished. People were just then engaged in collecting the arms that had been thrown away by the fugitives, and they had already formed a pile of them far exceeding the height of a man.

The smoking ruins of whole villages and towns, or extensive tracts laid waste by inundations, exhibit a melancholy spectacle; but a field of battle is assuredly the most shocking sight that eye can ever behold. Here all kinds of horrors are united; here Death reaps his richest harvest, and revels amid a thousand different forms of human suffering. The whole area has of itself a peculiar and repulsive physiognomy, resulting from such a variety of heterogeneous objects as are nowhere else found together. The relics of torches, the littered and trampled straw, the bones and flesh of slaughtered animals, fragments of plates, a thousand articles of leather, tattered cartouche boxes, old rags, clothes thrown away, all kinds of harness, broken muskets, shattered wagons and carts, weapons of all sorts, thousands of dead and dying, horribly mangled bodies of men and horses,— and all these intermingled!

I shudder whenever I recall to memory this scene, which, for the world, I would not again behold. Such, however, was the spectacle that presented itself in all directions; so that a person, who had before seen the beautiful environs of Leipzig, would not have known them again in their present state. Barriers, gardens, parks, hedges, and walks, were alike destroyed and swept away. These devastations were not the consequence of this day's engagement, but of the previous bivouacking of the French, who are now so habituated to conduct themselves in such a manner that their bivouacs never fail to exhibit the most deplorable attestations of their presence, as to admit no hopes of a change.

The appearance of Richter's garden was a fair specimen of the aspect of all the others. Among these the beautiful one of Löhr was particularly remarkable. Here French artillery had been stationed towards Göhlis; and here both horses and men had suffered most severely. The magnificent buildings, in the Grecian style, seemed mournfully to overlook their late agreeable, now devastated, groves, enlivened in spring by the warbling of hundreds of nightingales, but where now nothing was to be heard, save the loud groans of the dying. The dark alleys, summer-houses, and arbours, so often resorted to for recreation, social pleasures, or silent meditation, were now the haunts of death, the abode of agony and despair. The gardens, so late a paradise, were transformed into the seat of corruption and pestilential putridity. A similar spectacle was exhibited by Grosbosch's, Reichel's, and all the other spacious gardens round the city, which the allies had been obliged to storm.

The buildings which had suffered most were those at the outer gates of the city. These were the habitations of the excise and other officers stationed at the gates. Most of them were so perforated as rather to resemble large cages, which you may see through, than solid walls. All this, however, though more than a thousand balls must have been fired at the city, bore no comparison to the mischiefs which might have ensued, and which we had every reason to apprehend. We now look forward to a happier futurity; the commerce of Leipzig will revive; and the activity, industry, and good taste of its inhabitants, will, doubtless, ere long, call forth from these ruins a new and more beautiful creation.

I now summon your attention from these scenes of horror to others of a different kind, the delineation of which is absolutely necessary to complete the picture. Those hosts which had so long been the scourge of Germany and Europe, and had left us this last hideous monument of their presence, perhaps never to return, were now in precipitate flight, as though hurried away by an impetuous torrent. The terrors of the Most High had descended upon them. The conqueror had appeared to them at Leipzig in the most terrific form, and with uplifted arm followed close at their heels. About a league beyond the city the ardour of the pursuit somewhat abated; at Markranstädt the routed army first stopped to take breath, and to form itself in some measure into a connected whole.

The booty taken by the allies was immense. The suburbs were crowded with wagons and artillery, which the enemy had been obliged to abandon. It was impossible for the most experienced eye to form any kind of estimate of their numbers. The captors left them all just as they were, and merely examined here and there the contents of the wagons. Many of them were laden with rice, which was partly given away, especially by the Prussians. Many a Frenchman probably missed the usual supply of it for his scanty supper. All the streets were thronged with the allied troops, who had fought dispersed, and now met to congratulate one another on the important victory. Soon after the city was taken, their sovereigns made their entry. The people pressed in crowds to behold their august and so long wished-for deliverers. They appeared without any pomp in the simplest officers' uniforms, attended by those heroes, Blücher, Bülow, Platow, Barklay de Tolly, Schwarzenberg, Repnin, Sanders, &c. &c., whom we had so long admired. The acclamations of the people were unbounded. Tens of thousands of voices greeted them with *Huzzas* and *Vivats*; and white handkerchiefs,—symbols of peace,—waved from every window. Some few indeed were too unhappy to take part in the general joy on this memorable day. It was the only punishment, but truly a severe one, for the abject wretches who have not German hearts in their bosoms. Never did acclamations so sincere greet the ears of emperors and kings as those which welcomed Alexander, Francis, Frederic William, and Charles John. They were followed by long files of troops, who had so gloriously sustained the arduous contest under their victorious banners. In the midst of Cossacks, Prussian, Russian, Austrian, and Swedish hussars, appeared also our gallant Saxon cavalry, resolved henceforward to fight for the liberty of Germany, and the genuine interests of their native land.

A great number of regiments immediately continued their march without halting, and took some the road to Pegau, and others that to Merseburg, in order to pursue the enemy in his left flank and in his rear. Blücher's army had the preceding day advanced to the neighbourhood of Merseburg, where it was now posted in the right flank of the retreating force. Leipzig had nothing more to fear. French officers and soldiers were everywhere seen intermixed with their conquerors. It was only here and there that they were collected together and conveyed away. Of the greater part but little notice was taken in the first bustle, as all the gates were well guarded, and it was scarcely possible for one of them to escape. Numbers had fled during the assault from their quarters into the suburbs. Many seemed to have left behind valuable effects and money, as I should conjecture from various expressions used by some, who offered, several Napoleon-*d'ors* to any person who could assist them to reach their lodgings. For this, however, it was now too late. Strict orders were issued against the secreting or entertaining of Frenchmen, and they were therefore obliged to seek, for the moment, a refuge in the hospitals.

Only a small part of the combined troops had gone in pursuit of the French. By far the greatest portion reposed in countless ranks round the town from the fatigues of the long and sanguinary conflict. Part of the army equipage entered, and all the streets were soon crowded to such excess that you could scarcely stir but at the risk of your life. The allied monarchs alighted in the market-place, where the concourse of guards and equipages was consequently immense. Here I saw the late French commandant of the city coming on foot with a numerous retinue of officers and commissaries, and advancing towards the Russian generals. The fate of General Bertrand was certainly most to be pitied; he was a truly honest man, who had no share in those inexpressible miseries in which we had been for the last six months involved. I felt so much the less for the commissaries, whom I have ever considered as the Pandora's box of the French army, whence such numberless calamities have spread over every country in which they have set foot. At the residence of our sovereign I observed no other alteration than that a great number of Saxon generals and officers were collected about it. The life grenadier-guards were on duty as before, and a battalion of Russian grenadiers was parading in front of the windows. No interview, that I know of, took place between the King of Saxony the allied sovereigns. The King of Prussia remained here longest in conversation with the prince-royal. The emperors of Austria and Russia, as well as the Crown-Prince of Sweden, returned early to the army. After the departure of the Prussian monarch, our king set out under a strong escort of Cossacks for Berlin, or, as some asserted, for Schwedt.

The French hospitals which we had constantly had here since the beginning of the year, and which, since the battle of Lützen and the denunciation of the armistice, had increased to such a degree as to contain upwards of 20,000 sick and wounded, may be considered as a malignant cancer, that keeps eating farther and farther, and consuming the vital juices. It was these that introduced among us a dreadfully destructive nervous fever, which had increased the mortality of the inhabitants to near double its usual amount. Regarded in this point of view alone, they were one of the most terrible scourges of the city; but they proved a still more serious evil, inasmuch as the whole expense of them fell upon the circle. The French never inquired whence the prodigious funds requisite for their maintenance were to be derived, nor ever thought of making the smallest compensation. If we reckon, for six months, 10,000 sick upon an average, and for each of them 12 *groschen* per day (and, including all necessaries, they could scarcely be kept at that rate), the amount for each day is 5000, and, for the six months, the enormous sum of 900,000 dollars, which the exhausted coffers were obliged to pay in specie. This calculation, however, is so far below the truth, that it ought rather to be greatly augmented. A tolerable aggregate must have been formed by proportional contributions from all our country towns, and this was for the service of the hospitals alone: judge then of the rest.

Previously to the battle of Leipzig the state of the inmates of these pestilential dens, these abodes of misery, was deplorable enough, as they were continually becoming more crowded and enlarged. Many of the persons attached to them, and in particular many a valuable and experienced medical man, carried from them the seeds of death into the bosom of his family. With their want of accommodations, cleanliness was a point which could not be attained, and it was impossible to pass them without extreme disgust. As Leipzig was for a considerable time cut off from the rest of the world by the vast circle of armies, like the mariner cast upon a desert island, the wants of these hospitals became from day to day more urgent. Provisions also at length began to fail. The distress had arrived at its highest pitch, when the thousands from the field of battle applied there for relief. Not even bread could any longer be dispensed to these unfortunates. Many wandered about without any kind of shelter. Then did we witness scenes which would have thrilled the most obdurate cannibals with horror. No eye could have beheld a sight more hideous at Smolensk, on the Berezyna, or on the road to Wilna—there at least Death more speedily dispatched his victims. Thousands of ghastly figures staggered along the streets, begging at every window and at every door; and seldom indeed had compassion the power to give. These, however, were ordinary, familiar spectacles. Neither was it rare to see one of these emaciated wretches picking up the dirtiest bones, and eagerly gnawing them; nay, even the smallest crumb of bread which had chanced to be thrown into the street, as well as apple-parings and cabbage-stalks, were voraciously devoured. But hunger did not confine itself within these disgusting limits. More than twenty eye-witnesses can attest that wounded French soldiers crawled to the already putrid carcasses of horses, with some blunt knife or other contrived with their feeble hands to cut the flesh from the haunches, and greedily regaled themselves with the carrion. They were glad to appease their hunger with what the raven and the kite never feed on but in cases of necessity. They even tore the flesh from human limbs, and broiled it to satisfy the cravings of appetite; nay, what is almost incredible, the very dunghills were searched for undigested fragments to devour. You know me, and must certainly believe that I would not relate as facts things which would be liable to be contradicted by the whole city. Thus the hospitals became a hot-bed of pestilence, from which the senses of hearing, smell, and sight, turned with disgust, and one of the most fatal of those vampires which had so profusely drained our vitals, and now dispensed destruction to those who had fed them and to the sick themselves.

The great church-yard exhibited a spectacle of peculiar horror. The peaceful dead and their monuments had been spared no more than any other corner of the city. Here also the king of terrors had reaped a rich harvest. The slight walls had been converted into one great fort, and loop-holes formed in them. Troops had long before bivouacked in this spot, and the Prussian, Russian, and Austrian prisoners, were here confined, frequently for several successive days, in the most tempestuous weather and violent rain, without food, straw, or shelter. These poor fellows had nevertheless spared the many handsome monuments of the deceased, and only sought a refuge from the wet, or a lodging for the night, in such vaults as they found open. This spacious ground, which rather resembled a superbly embellished garden than a burial-place, now fell under the all-desolating hands of the French. It soon bore not the smallest resemblance to itself; what Art had, in the space of a century, employed a thousand hands to produce, was in a short time, and by very few, defaced and destroyed. The strongest iron doors to the vaults were broken open, the walls stripped of their decorations and emblems of mourning, the last tributes of grief and affection annihilated, and every atom of wood thrown into the watch-fire; so that the living could no longer know where to look for the remains of the deceased objects of their love. The elegant rails, with which the generality of the graves were encompassed, for the most part disappeared, and the only vestiges of them to be found were their ashes, or the relics of the reeking brands of the watch-fire. On the 19th this wretched bulwark also was stormed, and thrown down as easily as a fowler's net. The carcasses of horses now replaced upon the graves the monuments of mourning for the peaceful dead. After the battle part of the French prisoners were confined in this place. The church of St. John, which stands in it, had, as early as the month of May, been converted into an hospital, which, ever since the beginning of October, was crowded with sick. It could hold no more; the sick and prisoners were therefore intermingled, and lay down pell-mell among the graves. What had hitherto been spared was now completely destroyed. In this case, indeed, dire necessity pleaded a sufficient excuse. Who could find fault with distress and despair if they resorted to the only means that could afford them the slightest alleviation? Who could grudge them a shelter in the cold autumnal nights, even though they sought it in the dreary abode of mouldering corpses? Every vault which it was possible for them to open was converted into a chamber and dwelling-place, which at least was preferable to a couch between hillocks soaked with rain or covered with hoar frost. They descended into the deepest graves, broke open the coffins, and ejected their tenants, to procure fire-wood to warm their frozen limbs. I myself saw a French soldier who had fallen among a heap of coffins piled up to the height of more than twelve feet; and, unable to clamber up again, had probably lain there several days, and been added by Death to the number of his former victims. The appearance of the skulls, before so carefully concealed from the view of the living, now thrown out of the coffins into the graves, was truly ghastly.

In spite of all the exertion of the new authorities, appointed by the allies to alleviate the general misery, it was utterly impossible for any human power to restore order in the horrid chaos which the French had left behind them. A severe want of all necessaries was felt in the city; the circumjacent villages, far and wide, were plundered and laid waste. From them, of course, no supply could be obtained. More than thirty hospitals were not capable of receiving all the sick and wounded who applied for admission. Where were to be found buildings sufficiently spacious, mattresses, bedding, utensils, provisions, and the prodigious number of medical attendants, whose services were so urgently required by these poor creatures? Every edifice at all adapted to the purpose had long been occupied; and so completely had everything been drained by requisitions, that the hospital committee had for some time been unable to collect even the necessary quantity of lint. Almost every barber's apprentice was obliged to exercise his unskilful hands in the service of the hospitals. It would have been impossible to procure anything with money, had it been ever so plentiful; and this resource, moreover, was already completely exhausted. The most acute understanding and the most invincible presence of mind were inadequate to the providing of a remedy for these evils. Nowhere was there to be seen either beginning or end. The city was covered with carcasses, and the rivers obstructed with dead bodies. Thousands of hands were necessary to remove and bury these disgusting objects before any attention could be paid to the clearing of the field of battle about Leipzig. As all sought relief, there was of course none to afford it. It was difficult to decide whether first to build, to slaughter, to brew, to bake, to bury the dead, or to assist the wounded, as all these points demanded equally prompt attention.

In the city lay many thousands of newly-arrived troops, who came from the fight, and were both hungry and thirsty. Notwithstanding their moderation, some of these could obtain nothing, and others but a very scanty supply. Gladly would every citizen have entertained them in the best manner; but not even a glass of the worst beer or brandy was now to be had. Many of them naturally ascribed this to ill will, and even observed that everything was denied them because they were not Frenchmen. How little did they know of our real situation! In the house where I live six of the Prussian foot-guards were quartered. They com-

plained when nothing was set before them but dry potatoes; but listened with calmness to the excuses that were
offered. Without making any reply, four of them took up
their arms, and departed. In about an hour they returned,
bringing with them two cows, which they had taken from
the French. These they presented to their host, and immediately fell to work and killed then. In two hours the family
was abundantly supplied with meat, so that it could assist
others; and, as great part was pickled, it was supplied for
a considerable time. Frenchmen would certainly not have
acted thus.

Among the thousands of facts which might be adduced
to prove that it was absolutely impossible for anything
whatever to be left in the town, that its resources were
completely exhausted, and that extreme want could not but
prevail, let one instance suffice. There were in the city two
granaries, one of which, in the palace of Pleissenburg, had
been filled at the king's cost, and the other, called the corn-
magazine, at the expense of the magistrates. The former
had long been put in requisition by French commissaries,
and had been chiefly applied to the provisioning of the
French garrisons of Wittenberg and Torgau. As this was the
king's property, it was perhaps but right to demand it for
the fortresses which were to defend the country. The stores
possessed by the magistrates were purchased in those years
when a scarcity of corn prevailed in Saxony. To afford some
relief the government had imported great quantities from
Russia, by way of the Baltic and the Elbe. The magistrates
of Leipzig had bought a considerable part of it, that they
might be able to relieve the wants of the citizens in case a
similar calamity should again occur. It was ground and put
into casks, each containing 450 pounds. They had in their
magazine 4000 such casks, which had been left untouched
even in the year 1806, and were carefully preserved, to be

used only in cases of extreme necessity. This was certainly a wise and truly paternal precaution. So valuable a store would have been sufficient to protect the city from hunger for a considerable time. As the French army behaved all over Saxony as though it had been in an enemy's country, and consumed everything far and near, the most urgent want was the inevitable consequence. They forgot the common maxim, that the bread of which you deprive the citizen and the husbandman is in fact taken from yourself, and that the soldier can have nothing where those who feed him have lost their all. The country round Dresden was already exhausted. Soldiers and travellers coming from that quarter could scarcely find terms to describe the distress. They unanimously declared that the country from Oschatz to Leipzig was a real paradise, in comparison with Lusatia and the circle of Misnia, as far as the Elbe. Of this we soon had convincing proofs. It was necessary to pick out a great number of horses from all the regiments, and to send back numerous troops of soldiers to the depots. Don Quixote's Rosinante was a superb animal compared with those which returned to Dresden. Most of them had previously perished by the way. Here they covered all the streets. The men sold them out of hand, partly for a few *groschen*. A great number were publicly put up to auction by the French commissaries; and you may form some idea what sorry beasts they must have been, when you know that a lot of 26 was sold for 20 dollars. After some time the whole of the horse-guards arrived here. They were computed at 5000 men, all of whom were unfit for service. How changed! how lost was their once imposing appearance! Scarcely could troops ever make so ludicrous, so grotesque, and so miserable a figure. Gigantic grenadiers, with caps of prodigious height, and heavy-armed cuirassiers, were seen riding upon lean cows, which certainly did not cut many capers. It was wonderful that the animals showed no disposition to decline the singular honour. Their knapsacks were fastened to the horns, so that you were puzzled to make out what kind of a monstrous creature was approaching. Carbineers, with cuirasses and helmets polished like mirrors, lay without boots and stockings in wheelbarrows, to which a peasant had harnessed himself with his dog, and thus transported the heroes. Few of the horses were yet able to carry the knapsack, and much less the rider. The men were therefore obliged to drag the jaded beasts by the bridle through the deepest morasses, and thought themselves fortunate when at last the animals dropped to rise no more. Compared with these endless caravans, a band of strolling players might be considered as the triumphant procession of a Roman emperor. All these men were proceeding to Erfurt and Mentz.

These, and similar scenes which we had daily witnessed, were a natural consequence of the French system of supply, and the prodigious bodies of troops, which bore no proportion to the resources of a small tract of country. Attempts had been made, but without success, to find other provinces abounding in grain and forage. The fertile fields of Silesia and Bohemia were beyond their reach. The angel with the fiery sword vigilantly guarded the avenues to them against the fallen children of Adam. It was now absolutely necessary to devise some expedient; and to the French all means were alike. Some rice had been procured by way of the Elbe and the Rhine. The stocks in the warehouses of the tradesmen of Leipzig were now put in requisition, and sent off to the army; and I shrewdly suspect that no part of them was paid for. These, however, were but small privations; to relieve the general want required no less a miracle than that by which 1000 men were fed with five small loaves. The valuable stores in the city magazine had not yet been discovered. But where is the door, however strong, through which their eagle eyes would not at last penetrate? The flour was soon spied out, and forthwith destined for the hungry stomachs of the French. The barrels were rolled away with incredible expedition, and conveyed to the bakehouses. Each baker was supplied with two a day, which he was obliged to make up with all possible dispatch into bread, and to carry to the Cloth-hall. Here the loaves were piled up in immense rows, and sent off to the famishing army. From morning till night nothing was to be seen but wagons loading and setting out. Not a morsel, however, was given to the soldiers quartered upon the citizens; their superiors well knew that the patient landlord had yet a penny left in his pocket to help himself out with. Thus the fine magazine was stripped; and its valuable contents, which would have kept twenty years longer without spoiling, and had been preserved with such care, were dissipated in a moment. You may easily conceive how severe a misfortune this loss proved to the city, and how keenly it was felt, when you know that we were in a manner besieged for several weeks, and that not a handful of flour was to be had even at the mills themselves.

If you now take into the account the state of the city in a financial point of view, you may judge how dreadful its condition in general must have been. In no town is a better provision made for the indigent than in Leipzig. Here were poor-houses, under most judicious regulations, where food, fire, and lodging, were afforded. These buildings were converted into hospitals, their inmates were obliged to turn out, and at length the necessitous were deprived of their scanty allowance—the funds were exhausted, and no fresh supplies received. The citizen sunk under the weight of his burdens; it was impossible to lay any new ones upon him. Among the different sources of income enjoyed by the city, the author knows of one which at each of the two principal fairs commonly produced 4000 dollars; whereas the receipts from it at the late Michaelmas fair fell short of 100 dollars. All the other branches of revenue, whether belonging to the king or to the city, fared no better.

Such was the state of a city, which a few years since might justly be numbered among the most opulent in Germany, and whose resources appeared inexhaustible. It may be considered as the heart of all Saxony, on account of the manifold channels for trade, manufactures, and industry, which here meet as in one common centre. Hence the commerce of Saxony extends to every part of the globe. With the credit of Leipzig, that of all Saxony could not fail to be in a great measure destroyed. Had this state of things continued a little longer, absolute ruin would probably have ensued, as the total suspension of trade would certainly have occasioned the removal of all the yet remaining moneyed men. So low, however, the city was not destined to fall. The fatal blow already impended over Leipzig, which was on the point of being reduced to a heap of ashes. Black storm-clouds gathered thick around it; but they passed off; and a new sun, the cheering hope of better times, burst forth. Large bodies of troops are yet within our walls; and they are a heavy burden to the impoverished inhabitants, under their present circumstances. We shall, however, be relieved of some part of it, on the reduction of the fortresses upon the Elbe, which the enemy may yet defend for some time, though without any other prospect than that of final surrender, and of wielding for the last time his desolating arms on the shores of that river. Symptoms of reviving trade and commerce begin at least to appear. The gates are no longer beset with the Argus eyes of French inspectors. The patient indeed, brought as he has been to the very gates of death, is yet extremely weak, and requires the aid of crutches. Long will it be before he is free from pain, but his recovery is sure: he has quitted the close sick room, and is now consigned to better care, to the hands of Prudence and Philanthropy, who are acquainted with his condition, and will infallibly restore him to his former health and vigour.

The Confederation of the Rhine and the Continental system,—terms synonymous with all the evils which have brought Germany and Europe to the brink of destruction,—will in future have no other signification in the vocabularies of the writers on political economy than that interval of severe probation when Germany seemed to be annihilated, but yet rose from her ruins with renewed energies, and, united more firmly than ever, by new ties, with the other states of Europe, resumed her ancient rights. The battle of Leipzig was the watch-word for this great revolution. History, therefore, when partiality and passion shall have long been silent, will not fail to class it among the most important events recorded in her annals.

Here permit me to conclude my letters respecting those eventful days of October, which must ever be so deeply impressed upon the memories of us all. What may be called the military part of my narrative may be imperfect; the names of the generals who commanded, the positions of particular corps, and other circumstances of minor importance, may perhaps be incorrect; yet the circumstantial details which I have given will enable you to form to yourself in some measure a complete picture of that memorable conflict.

An Overview

In the battle of Leipzig the reflecting observer discovers something grand; but there is also much that puzzles one who is not a soldier, and is accustomed to find in all Napoleon's campaigns a consistency of plan which he here looks for in vain. If in his earlier combinations he did not in every instance take all possibilities into the account, but overlooked some, this must be ascribed not so much to the want of military penetration, as to his firm confidence in his good fortune, and in his ability to turn unforeseen accidents to his own advantage, or at least to render them harmless. Rarely has a general been so highly favoured by fortune for a long series of years as he.

It is no wonder then that this confidence at length increased to such a degree as frequently to become the height of temerity. In Russia, Napoleon met with many circumstances which he had not taken into his calculation; but he nevertheless penetrated to Moscow. Here he for the first time experienced such a reverse as no general ever yet sustained. His immense army was entirely annihilated. His stern decree created a new one, to all outward appearance equally formidable.

From the haste with which its component parts were collected, it could not but be deficient in intrinsic energy, and it was impossible to doubt that this would be shown in time. In this respect his antagonists had a decided advantage, as must have been obvious to him after the battles of Lützen and Bautzen. Had he not been so vastly superior in number to the Russian and Prussian army in the first engagement, he would indisputably have been defeated on that occasion.

The political relations of Europe had moreover undergone an extraordinary change. He could not for a thousand reasons be a moment doubtful of the choice of Austria. If with a strong and well-appointed army she could not by negotiation bring about a peace upon the basis of a future balance of power among the principal states of Europe, in which Prussia and Russia were willing to acquiesce, there could be no question that for the sake of her own existence she would espouse the cause of those two powers.

This Napoleon seems to have considered as impossible, or the advantages already obtained must have inspired him with the confidence that even the accession of Austria to the alliance could not prevent the prosecution of his victorious career to the Vistula. Could he have expected to encounter the whole Austrian army in Silesia, or to reduce the fortresses of Upper Silesia, with such rapidity as to be able a third time to menace Vienna, and to compel the force assembled on the Bohemian frontiers to return with precipitation to cover the capital? This would have been too presumptuous an idea. He probably fancied himself strong enough, with 400,000 men, led on by himself and the ablest generals of the age, to cope, if even Austria should declare against him, with all three powers; especially if he presumed that he should be able to force all the combined armies united to a general engagement, and to annihilate them with a single blow.

The proposals for peace were rejected: not the slightest

disposition was shown to treat, and the armistice of two months answered no other purpose than to convince Austria of the absolute necessity of joining the cause of the allies, and exerting all her energies to conquer that peace by the sword, which there was not the least hope of accomplishing by negotiation. By the accession of Austria the grand alliance had now gained a manifest superiority, as well in regard to the number of troops as to the geographical advantages of the theatre of war and resources. After the renewal of hostilities Napoleon still seemed determined to pursue his plan of advancing beyond the Oder.

The allies were not to be deceived by these demonstrations, but unexpectedly took post with their main force in Bohemia, along the Saxon frontier, leaving in Silesia and Brandenburg, where the crown-prince of Sweden had by this time arrived with his gallant troops, armies strong enough to keep him in check by a vigorous defensive system. The great Bohemian army was destined for offensive operations. This plan was equally grand and judicious. Silesia, and all Saxony, to the Elbe, could not fail, in consequence, to be lost to Napoleon. That river, while he had only Prussia and Russia to encounter, was a sure support in his rear; but no sooner had Austria declared herself than it was no longer of any military consequence. Dresden was the central point for the French army.

There were organized all the military bureaus, and all the branches of administration for the economy of the army. The allies opened the campaign with a hasty advance upon that important city. If the enterprise proved successful, its consequences would be incalculable; if it miscarried, nothing would be lost for the grand object; and at any rate the expedition would be a diversion, which would immediately draw the French out of Silesia. Napoleon now saw how egregiously he was deceived in his reckoning. He hastened precipitately to save the Saxon capital. The army arrived breathless. The allies were already assaulting the suburbs; and, had Napoleon come one hour later, Dresden would have been in their power. Owing to the unexpected appearance of so prodigious a force, and still more to physical accidents, the grand enterprise of the allies miscarried.

The battle of Dresden terminated to their disadvantage, but their primary object was attained. Napoleon's force was divided into three great armies. Should any of them sustain a defeat, all Saxony to the right of the Elbe would be lost to him. The engagements of Jauer, Grossbeeren, and Dennewitz, proved disastrous to the French generals, and Lusatia and the right bank of the Elbe were soon in the hands of the allies. All the attempts to penetrate to Prague and Berlin ended in the discomfiture and annihilation of whole French corps. Oudinot, Ney, Regnier, Bertrand, and the terrible Vandamme, were in succession so totally defeated, that it was not possible even for the French reporters, with all their address, to cloak their disasters.

The allies everywhere acted offensively. Saxony, surrounded by Silesia, Bohemia, and Brandenburg, was now, from its situation, likely to become, earlier or later, the grave of the French armies: the allies had every where the choice of their operations; they were neither to be turned nor broken through. It was evident that the long and obstinate continuance of Napoleon at Dresden could not fail to prove ruinous to him.

Of what service could the Elbe be to him, when Bohemia, the key to that river, was in the hands of his opponents? These had it in their power to turn his flank as far as the Saale, without hazard or any great impediment, as the event actually proved. Napoleon was cooped up in a narrow space, where in time, even without being defeated, he would have been in danger of starving with his army. Dresden was to him, in some respects, what Wilna had been in 1812. Leipzig, an open place, was now of far greater importance to him than Minsk was then. How easily might he have lost it, as the allies were advancing in considerable force upon that place! It was not lost, to be sure; but the communication between Dresden and Leipzig, and Leipzig and Erfurt, was, if not cut off, at least interrupted; his supplies became more and more precarious, and a large garrison, which it was deemed necessary to reinforce with strong detachments from the main army, was locked up in Leipzig.

When in August Austria declared herself decidedly in favour of Russia and Prussia, it was natural to expect that Napoleon would have totally relinquished the useless defence of Saxony, and have adopted a new plan of operations, in order to cover and preserve the other states of the confederation of the Rhine. That he would infallibly be compelled to evacuate Saxony, was evident from the slightest inspection of the map.

In this beautiful province he could expect no other glory than that of plunging it, by his inflexible obstinacy, into the most abject misery. The combined monarchs had nothing to fear for their own dominions; they needed to do no more than to carry on for some time a mere war of observation, and to recruit their forces. They might quietly await the moment when Napoleon should leave Dresden, and, on his arrival, force him to a general engagement in any situation which they should deem most advantageous.

Too late did Napoleon resolve upon retreat. He was obliged to commence it in the midst of an immense quadrangle which the allies formed about him, and to direct his course towards Leipzig. He could not, however, yet determine to give up Dresden, but left there a considerable army, thus weakening himself, and sacrificing it, as well as the garrisons of the fortresses on the Elbe and Oder, to no purpose whatever, in case he should lose a battle. At length, near Leipzig, he was forced, into the arduous conflict. Since the latter half of August, the talents which he had heretofore displayed for comprehensive and profound combinations seemed to have totally deserted him. All his measures and plans appeared imperfect, and betrayed a vacillation which he had never yet manifested. He seems to have been as uncertain respecting the strength of his antagonists as in regard to their grand plan of deciding the fate of the campaign with a single blow.

In the battle of Leipzig we perceive none of that forethought which characterizes his other engagements. The possibility of losing it seems never to have entered into his calculations; otherwise he would scarcely have endeavoured to prevail upon the king of Saxony to repair to Leipzig to witness his defeat. In the most favourable event he had a right to anticipate no other result than an unmolested retreat: the allies however, were producing a very different one from what he expected.

Of this he might have convinced himself so early as the 16th, when he encountered the strongest resistance at all points which he had probably deemed the weakest. From that day all his measures were calculated only for the moment. He boasted of victory when the battle was scarcely begun. He everywhere strove to check the impetuous advance of his foes at the expense of those means which were so necessary for his own retreat. It could not be difficult for Napoleon to foresee, on the 16th, that, in case he should be defeated, he had no other route left than to retreat westward, in the direction of Lützen and Merseburg.

He nevertheless caused all the bridges over the numerous muddy streams on that side to be destroyed, instead of diligently providing temporary ones in addition. He was acquainted with the situation of the city, through the centre of which he would be obliged to pass. He knew the position of his army, which might, indeed, enter it by three spacious roads, from north, east, and south; but had only one outlet, and this the very narrowest of all, for itself and its train, many miles in length. Let the reader figure to himself a routed army, and that a French army, in which all order is so easily lost, converging in three columns to one common centre.

The passage at the outermost gate towards Lützen is so narrow as to admit only one single wagon at a time. When we consider that at the Kuhthurm again the road is but just wide enough for one carriage; that, on the west side of the city, the Elster, the Pleisse, and their different branches, intersect with their thousand meanders the marshy plains covered with wood, which are scarcely passable for the pedestrian; when we farther consider the incessant stoppages of the whole train at every little obstacle, and figure to ourselves all the three columns united in a road, the two principal passes of which are scarcely 30 feet in breadth; we shall rather be astonished that the whole French army was not annihilated than surprised at the prodigious quantity of wagons and artillery which it was obliged to abandon.

Even in the night between the 18th and 19th, when Napoleon must have been perfectly aware of his situation, there would still have been time to throw bridges across the different streams, so that the army might have marched in five or six columns to Lindenau, and been again collected at this place, from which several convenient roads branch off. Such dispositions as circumstances required might then have been made, and the retreat might have been effected with inconsiderable loss. Such a precaution was the more necessary, as he could not be ignorant that Blücher's troops had already gained a march upon him, and was waiting for him at the Saale.

Thus the want of a few paltry wooden bridges proved as

ruinous to the French army as the battle itself. It lost, solely because it was unprovided with them, great part of its yet remaining artillery, several thousands of dead, who were mostly drowned, and a great number of prisoners. It was evident that such a retreat, conducted without order and without plan, was likely to be attended with the total destruction of the remnant of the army before it could reach the Rhine.

By the actions on the Unstrut and Saale, at Eisenach and Hanau, this force was actually so reduced, that, on its arrival at the Rhine, it must probably have entirely lost its military consequence. How infinitely inferior is Napoleon in this branch of the military art to the immortal Moreau, to whom he would have owed everlasting obligations, had he, at his glorious death, bequeathed to him the transcendent art of converting retreats into victories!

In regard to boldness, Napoleon certainly belongs to the generals of the first rank. He has undertaken and executed the rashest enterprises. But, if the true hero shines with the greatest lustre in misfortune, like Hannibal and Frederic the Great, Napoleon must be classed far below them. He abandoned his army in Russia when it had most need of his assistance; and the reason assigned for this desertion—that circumstances rendered his presence necessary in France— is by no means satisfactory to the rigid inquirer.

During the Seven-Years' War, the more dangerous the situation of the Prussian army, the more Frederic felt himself bound to continue with it, and to assist it with his eminent military genius. The campaign of 1813 has clearly proved that the secret of Napoleon's most decisive victories has consisted in the art of assailing his opponents with a superior force. Napoleon would be incapable of attacking with 30,000 men an army of 90,000, posted in an advantageous position, and defeating it, as Frederic did at Leuthen. Napoleon, like the Prussian monarch, attempted to penetrate into Bohemia, a country so dangerous for an army; but what a wretched business did he make of it, in comparison with the latter! Frederic waged war that he might conquer peace; Napoleon never wished for peace, often as he has made a show of desiring it. Frederic knew how to stop his victorious career in time, for History had taught him that it is as difficult to retain as to acquire glory. Napoleon imagined that his fame was susceptible of increase alone, and lost it all in the fields of Leipzig. The hardly-earned laurels of France faded along with it.

With what feelings must he direct his views beyond the Rhine, where the eyes of so many thousands are now opened? He too has lived to witness days which are far from agreeable to him. He, who represented it to the countries which he forced into his alliance as a supreme felicity to have their sons led forth to fight foreign battles, and to have many thousands of them sacrificed every year upon the altar of his ambition, now sees them all abandon him, and become his bitterest enemies.

The Great Empire is now an idle dream. Already is he nearly confined within that ancient France, which has lost through him the flower of her population. Long has discontent lurked there in every bosom; long have her people beheld with indignation their youth driven across the Rhine, into foreign lands, where they were swept away by cold, famine, and the sword, so that few of them revisited their paternal homes. Will the nation again be ready to bathe foreign plains with the blood of half a million of fresh victims? Scarcely can it be so infatuated.

The French too are now roused from their torpor: like the Germans, they will confine their exertions to the defence of their own frontiers against those mighty armies of Europe, which, crowned with laurels, wield the sword in one hand, and bear the olive of peace in the other.

A Conversation with Napoleon

The following letter, which cannot but be considered as most honourable to the writer, contains so many minute, but, at the same time, highly characteristic traits, that it cannot fail to prove extremely interesting to every reader. No other apology is necessary for its introduction here.

Leipzig
November 3, 1813
Dearest Friend,
You here see how ready I am to gratify your desire of knowing everything that passed in my neighbourhood and that befell myself in the eventful days of October. I proceed to the point without farther preamble.

Ever since the arrival of marshal Marmont I have constantly resided at the beautiful country-house of my employer at R★★★, where I imagined that I might be of some service during the impending events. The general of brigade Chamois, an honest man, but a severe officer, was at first quartered there.

On the 14th of October everybody expected a general engagement near Leipzig. On that day several French corps had arrived in the neighbourhood. The near thunders of the artillery, which began to roll, and the repeated assurances of the French officers that the anniversary of the battles of Ulm and Jena would not be suffered to pass uncelebrated, seemed to confirm this expectation. The King of Saxony entered by the *palisadoed* gates of the outer city, and Napoleon also soon arrived. The latter came from Düben, and took possession of a bivouac in the open field, not far from the gallows, close to a great watch-fire. I was one of those who hastened to the spot, to obtain a sight of the extraordinary man, little suspecting that a still greater honour awaited me, namely, that of sleeping under the same roof, nay, even of being admitted to a personal interview of some length with him. The state of things at my country-house did not permit me to be long absent. I hastened back, therefore, with all possible expedition. I arrived nearly at the same moment with a French *marechal de logis du palais*, to whom I was obliged to show every apartment in the house, and who, to my no small dismay, announced "that the emperor would probably lodge there that night." The man, having despatched his errand in great haste, immediately departed. I communicated the unexpected intelligence to the aid-de-camp of general Pajol, but expressly observed that I had great doubts about it, as the *marechal de logis* himself had not spoken positively. The aid-de-camp appeared very uneasy; and, though I strove to convince him that it must be some time before our distinguished guest could arrive, he immediately packed up, and, notwithstanding all my earnest endeavours to detain him, he was gone with his servant in a few minutes. Seldom have I witnessed such an extraordinary degree of anxiety as this man showed while preparing for his departure.

The *marechal de logis* soon returned, and again inspected all the apartments, and even the smallest closets, more minutely than before. He announced that *sa majesté* would certainly take up his head-quarters here, and asked for a piece of chalk, to mark each room with the names of the distinguished personages by whom they were to be occupied. When he had shown me the apartment destined for the emperor, he desired that a fire might be immediately lighted in it, as his majesty was very fond of warmth. The bustle soon began; the guards appeared, and occupied the house and all the avenues. Many officers of rank, with numerous attendants, arrived; and six of the emperor's cooks were soon busily engaged in the kitchen. Thus I was soon surrounded on all sides with imperial splendour, and might consider myself for the moment as its centre. I might possibly have felt no small degree of vanity on the occasion, had I not been every instant reminded that the part which I should have to act would be that of obedience alone. I heard the beating of drums at a distance, which, as I presently learned, announced that I was shortly to descend into a very subordinate station. It proclaimed the arrival of the emperor, who came on horseback in a grey *surtout*. Behind him rode the Duke of Vicenza (Caulincourt), who, since the death of Marshal Duroc, has succeeded to his office. When they had come up to the house, the master of the horse sprung from his steed with a lightness and agility which I should not have expected in such a raw-boned, stiff-looking gentleman, and immediately held that of the emperor.

His Majesty had scarcely reached his apartments when I was hastily sought and called for. You may easily conceive my astonishment and perturbation when I was told that the emperor desired to speak with me immediately. Now, in such a state of things, I had not once thought for several days of putting on my Sunday clothes; but, to say nothing of this, my mind was still less prepared for an interview with a hero, the mere sight of whom was enough to bow me down to the very ground. In this emergency courage alone could be of any service, and I rallied my spirits as well as the short notice would permit. I had done nothing amiss—at least that I knew of—and had performed my duty as *maître d'hotel* to the best of my ability. After a general had taken charge of me, I mustered my whole stock of rhetorical flourishes, best calculated to win the favour of a mighty emperor. The general conducted me through a crowd of aid-de-camps and officers of all ranks. They took but little notice of such an insignificant being, and indeed scarcely deigned to bestow a look upon me. My conductor opened the door, and I entered with a heart throbbing violently. The emperor had pulled off his *surtout*, and had nobody with him. On the long table was spread a map of prodigious size. Rustan, the Mameluke, who has so long been falsely reported to be dead, was, as I afterwards learned, in the next room.

My presence of mind was all gone again when I came to be introduced to the emperor, and he must certainly have perceived by my looks that I was not a little confused. I was just going to begin the harangue which I had studied with such pains, and to stammer out something or other about the high and unexpected felicity of being presented to the most powerful, the most celebrated, and the most sincerely beloved monarch in the world, when he relieved me at once from my dilemma. He addressed me in French, speaking very quick, but distinctly, to the following effect:

"Are you the master of this house?" Napoleon asked.

"No, please your majesty, only a servant." I replied.

"Where is the owner?"

"He is in the city. He is advanced in years; and under the present circumstances has quitted his house leaving me to take care of it as well as I can."

"What is your master?"

"He is in business, sire."

"In what line?"

"He is a banker."

"Oho! then he is worth a plum, (*un millionaire,*) I suppose?" Said Napoleon, laughing.

"Begging your majesty's pardon, indeed he is not."

"Well then, perhaps he may be worth two?"

"Would to God I could answer your majesty in the affirmative."

"You lend money, I presume?"

"Formerly we did, sire; but now we are glad to borrow."

"Yes, yes, I dare say you do a little in that way yet. What interest do you charge?"

"We used to charge from 4 to 5 per cent.; now we would willingly give from 8 to 10."

"To whom were you used to lend money?"

"To inferior tradesmen and manufacturers."

"You discount bills too, I suppose?"

"Formerly, sire, we did; now we can neither discount nor get any discounted."

"How is business with you?"

"At present, your majesty, there is none doing."

"How so?"

"Because all trade is totally at a standstill."

"But have you not your fair just now?"

"Yes, but it is so only in name."

"Why?"

"As all communication has for a considerable time been suspended, and the roads are unsafe for goods, neither sellers nor buyers will run the risk of coming; and, besides, the greatest scarcity of money prevails in this country."

"So, so! What is the name of your employer?" Napoleon asked, (*taking much snuff*).

I mentioned his name.

"Is he married?"

"Yes, sire."

"Has he any children."

"He has, and they are married too."

"In what capacity are you employed by him?"

"As a clerk."

"Then you have a cashier too, I suppose?"

"Yes, sire, at your service."

"What wages do you receive?"

I mentioned a sum that I thought fit.

He now motioned with his hand, and I retired with a low bow.

During the whole conversation the emperor was in very good humour, laughed frequently, and took a great deal of snuff. After the interview, on coming out of the room, I appeared a totally different and highly important person to all those who a quarter of an hour before had not deigned to take the slightest notice of me. Both officers and domestics now showed me the greatest respect. The emperor lodged in the first floor; his favourite Mameluke, an uncommonly handsome man, was constantly about his person. The second floor was occupied by the prince of Neufchatel, who had a very sickly appearance, and the duke of Bassano, the emperor's secretary. On the ground floor

a front room was converted into a *sallon au service.*
Here were marshals Oudinot, Mortier, Ney, Reynier,
with a great number of generals, aid-de-camps, and
other officers in waiting, who lay at night upon straw,
crowded as close as herrings in a barrel. In the left
wing lodged the Duke of Vicenza, master of the horse;
and above him the physician to the emperor, whose
name, I think, was M. Yvan. The right wing was occupied by the *officiers du palais.* The smallest room was
turned into the bed-chamber of a general; and every
corner was so filled, that the servants and other attendants were obliged to sleep on the kitchen floor.
Upon my remonstrance to the valet of the *marechal
du palais* I was allowed to keep a small apartment for
my own use, and thought to guard myself against unwelcome intruders by inscribing with chalk my high
rank—*maitre de la maison*—in large letters upon the
door. At first the new-comers passed respectfully before my little cell, and durst scarcely venture to peep
in at the door; but it was not long before French curiosity overleaped this written barrier. For sometime
this place served my people and several neighbours in
the village as a protecting asylum at night.

The keys of the hay-loft and barns I was commanded to deliver to the emperor's *piqueur.*—I earnestly entreated him to be as sparing of our stores
as possible, supporting this request with a bottle of
wine,—which, under the present circumstance, was
no contemptible present. He knew how to appreciate
it, and immediately gave me a proof of his gratitude.
He took me aside, and whispered in my ear, "As long
as the emperor is here you are safe; but the moment
he is gone—and nobody can tell how soon that may
be—you will be completely stripped by the guards;

the officers themselves will then show no mercy. You had best endeavour to obtain a safeguard, for which you must apply to the duke of Vicenza."

This advice was not thrown away upon me: I immediately begged to speak with the *grand ecuyer*. I explained my business as delicately as possible, and be with great good humour promised to comply with my request. Determined to strike while the iron was hot, I soon, afterwards repeated my application in writing.

After the emperor's arrival there was no such thing as a moment's rest for me. Gladly would I have exchanged my high function, which placed me upon an equal footing with the first officers of the French court, for a night's tranquil slumber. *M. maitre de la maison* was every moment called for. As for shaving, changing linen, brushing clothes—that was quite out of the question. His guests had remarked his good will, and they imagined that his ability was capable of keeping pace with it. Luckily it never came into my head, whilst invested with my high dignity, to look into a glass, otherwise I should certainly not have known myself again, and Diogenes would have appeared a beau in comparison. As to danger of life, or personal ill-treatment, I was under no apprehension; for who would have presumed to lay hands on so important a personage, who was every moment wanted, and whose place it would have been absolutely impossible to supply?

I was much less concerned about all this than about the means of saving the property of my employer, as far as lay in my power. The danger of having everything destroyed was very great.

The French guards had kindled a large fire at a small distance from the house. The wind, being high, drove not only sparks but great flakes of fire towards it. The whole court-yard was covered with straw, which was liable every moment to set us all in flames. I represented this circumstance to an officer of high rank, and observed that the emperor himself would be exposed to very great risk; on which he ordered a grenadier belonging to the guards to go and direct it to be put out immediately. This man, an excessively grim fellow, refused without ceremony to carry the order.

"They are my comrades," said he: "it is cold—they must have a fire, and dare not go too far off—I cannot desire them to put it out."

What was to be done? I bethought myself of the duke of Vicenza, and applied directly to him. My representations produced the desired effect. He gave orders, and in a quarter of an hour the fire was out. I was equally fortunate in saving a building situated near the house. It had been but lately constructed and fitted up. The young guard were on the point of pulling it down, with the intention of carrying the wood to their bivouacs. Their design was instantly prevented, and one single piece of timber only was destroyed. A guard was sent to the place, to defend it from all farther attacks. It had been burned down only last summer, through the carelessness of some French dragoons.

Late at night the King of Naples came with his retinue from Stötteritz. He was attended by a black Othello, who seems to serve him in the same capacity as Rustan does his brother-in-law Napoleon.

By day-break the emperor started with all his retinue, and took the road to Wolkwitz. The King of Naples had already set out for the same place. All was quiet during the day, and towards night the emperor returned. Several French officers had asserted, the preceding night, that a general engagement would certainly take place on the 15th. How imperfectly they were acquainted with the state of things, I could perceive from many of their expressions. In their opinion the armies of the allies were already as good as annihilated. By the emperor's masterly manoeuvres, the Russians and Swedes—the latter, by the bye, had not yet come up—were according to them completely cut off from the Austrians. A *courier de l'empereur* was honest enough to tell me simply that they had done nothing all day but look at one another, but that there would be so much the warmer work on the morrow. Very early indeed on the morning of the 16th, I remarked preparations for the final departure of the emperor. The *maitre d'hôtel* desired a bill of the provisions furnished him. I had already made out one, but that would not do. It was necessary that the articles should be arranged under particular heads, and a distinct account of each given in. I ran short of time, patience, and paper. All excuses were unavailing, and there was no time to be lost. I readily perceived that all the elegance required in a merchant's counting-house would not be expected here, and accordingly dispensed with many little formalities. I wrote upon the first paper that came to hand, and my bills were the most miserable scraps that ever were seen. The amount was immediately paid. Finding that the *maitre d'hôtel* had not the least notion that it would be but reasonable to make some remuneration to the servants, who had been so assiduous in their attendance, I was uncivil enough to remind him of it. He then desired me to give him a receipt for 200 francs, which I immediately divided among the domestics; though he remarked that I ought to give each but three or four, at most. I also made out a distinct account for the forage, but this was not paid.

At length arrived the long wished-for *sauvegarde*. It consisted of three *gens d'armes d'elite*, who had a written order from the Baron de Lennep, *ecuyer* to the emperor, by virtue of which they were to defend my house and property from all depredations. I immediately took a copy of this important protection, and nailed it upon the door. The house was gradually evacuated; I was soon left alone with my guards, and sincerely rejoiced that Heaven had sent me such honest fellows. It was impossible, indeed, to be quite easy; the thunders of the cannon rolled more and more awfully, and I had frequent visits from soldiers. My brave *gens d'armes*, however, drove them all away, and I never applied in vain when I besought them to assist a neighbour in distress. I showed my gratitude as far as lay in my power, and at least took care that they wanted for nothing.

One of these three men went into the city, and returned in haste, bringing the news of a great victory. "*Vive l'empereur!*" cried he; "*la bataille est gagnée.*"

When I inquired the particulars, he related, in the most confident manner, that an Austrian prince had been taken, with 30,000 men, and that they were already singing *Te Deum* in the city. This story seemed extremely improbable to me, as the cannonade was at that moment rather approaching than receding from us. I expressed my doubts of the fact, and told him that the battle could not possibly be yet decided. The man, however, would not give up the point, but insisted that the intelligence was official. When I asked him if he had seen the captive prince and the 30,000

Austrians, as they must certainly have been brought into the city, he frankly replied that he had not. Several persons from the town had seen no more of them than he, so that I could give a shrewd guess what degree of credit was due to the story.

In the afternoon of the 17th Marshal Ney suddenly appeared at the door with a numerous retinue, and without ceremony took up his quarters in the house. I saw nothing of the emperor all that day, nor did any circumstance worthy of notice occur. On the 18th, at three in the morning, Napoleon came quite unexpectedly in a carriage. He went immediately to Marshal Ney, with whom he remained in conversation about an hour. He then hastened away again, and was soon followed by the marshal, whose servants stayed behind. His post must have been a very warm one; for before noon he sent for two fresh horses, and a third was fetched in the afternoon. The cannonade grow more violent, and gradually approached nearer. I became more and more convinced that the pompous story of the victory the day before was a mere *gasconade*. So early as twelve o'clock things seemed to be taking a very disastrous turn for the French. About this time they began to fall back very fast upon the city. Shouts of *Vive l'Empereur!* suddenly resounded from thousands of voices, and at this cry I saw the weary soldiers turn about and advance. Appearances nevertheless became still more alarming. The balls from the cannon of the allies already fell very near us. One of them indeed was rude enough to kill a cow scarcely five paces from me, and to wound a Pole.

The French all this time could talk of nothing but victories, with which Fortune had, most unfortunately, rendered them but too familiar. One messenger of victory followed upon the heels of another.

"General Thielemann," cried an *aid-de-camp*, "has just been taken, with 6000 men; and the emperor ordered him to be instantly shot on the field of battle."

The most violent abuse was poured forth upon the Saxons, and I now learned that great part of them had gone over to the allies in the midst of the engagement. Heartily as I rejoiced at the circumstance, I neverthe-less joined the French officers in their execrations. The concourse kept increasing; the wounded arrived in troops. Towards evening everything attested that the French were very closely pressed. A servant came at full gallop to inform us that Marshal Ney might shortly be expected, and that he was wounded. The whole house was instantly in an uproar.

"Mon Dieu, mon Dieu!"—cried one to another—*"le prince est blessé—quel malheur!"*

Soon after the marshal himself arrived; he was on foot, and supported by an aid-de-camp. Vinegar was hastily called for. The marshal had been wounded in the arm by a cannon-ball, and the pain was so acute that he could not bear the motion of riding.

The houses in the village were everywhere plun-dered, and the inhabitants kept coming in to solicit assistance. I represented their distress to an aid-de-camp, who only shrugged his shoulders, and gave the miserable consolation that it was now impossible for him to put a stop to the evil.

At length, early on the 19th, we appeared likely to get rid in good earnest of the monster by which we had been so dreadfully tormented. All the French hurried in disorder to the city, and our *sauvegarde* also made preparations to depart. Already did I again behold in imagination the pikes of the Cossacks. All the subsequent events followed in rapid succession. My *gens d'armes* were scarcely gone when a very brisk fire of sharp-shooters commenced in our neighbourhood. In a few moments Pomeranian infantry poured from behind through the garden into the house. They immediately proceeded, without stopping, to the city. It was only for a few minutes that I could observe with a glass the confused retreat of the French. Joy at the long wished-for arrival of our countrymen and deliverers soon called me away. The galling yoke was now shaken off, probably for ever. I bade a hearty welcome to the brave soldiers; and, as I saw several wounded brought in, I hastened to afford them all the assistance in my power. I may ascribe to my unwearied assiduity the preservation of the life of Lieutenant M——, a Swedish officer, who was dangerously wounded; and by means of it I had likewise the satisfaction to save the arm of the Prussian Captain Von B——, which, but for that, would certainly have required amputation. On the other hand, all my exertions in behalf of the Swedish Major Von Döbeln proved unavailing; I had the mortification to see him expire.

I was incessantly engaged with my wounded patients, while more numerous bodies of troops continued to hasten towards the town. We now thought ourselves fortunate in being already in the rear of the victorious army; but the universal cry was, 'What will become of poor Leipzig?' which was at this moment most furiously assaulted.

Various officers of distinction kept dropping in. The Swedish Adjutant-General Güldenskiöld arrived with the captive General Reynier, who alighted and took up his abode in the apartment in which the emperor had lodged. He was followed by the Prussian Colonel Von Zastrow, a most amiable man, and soon after the Prussian General Von Bülow arrived with his suite.

Our stock of provisions was almost entirely consumed, and you may conceive my vexation at being unable, with the best will in the world, to treat our ardently wished-for guests in a suitable manner. I had long been obliged to endure hunger myself, and to take it as an especial favour if the French cooks and valets had the generosity to allow me a small portion, of the victuals with which they were supplied.

At the very moment when Marshal Ney arrived, a fire had broken out in the neighbourhood, through the carelessness of the French. I hastened to the spot, to render assistance, if possible. It was particularly fortunate, considering the violence of the wind, and the want of means to extinguish the flames, that only two houses were destroyed. The fire-engines and utensils provided for such purposes had been carried off for fuel to the bivouacs. Such of the inhabitants of the village as had not run away, just now kept close in their houses, not daring to venture abroad. A number of unfeeling Frenchmen stood about gazing at the fire, without moving a finger towards extinguishing it. I called out to them to lend a hand to check the progress of the conflagration. A scornful burst of laughter was the only reply: the scoundrels would not stir, and absolutely could not contain their joy whenever the flames burned more furiously than usual. At the same time I witnessed proceedings, of which the wildest savage would not have been guilty. I saw these same wretches, who, a few days afterwards, voraciously devoured before my face the flesh of dead horses, and even human carcasses, wantonly trample bread, already so great a rarity, like brute beasts in the dirt.

For six or eight nights I had not been able to get a moment's sleep or rest, so that at last I reeled about like one drunk or stupid. The only wonder is that my health was not impaired by these super-human exertions. My dress and general appearance were frightful. When the wounded Swedish officer was brought in, he of course wanted a change of linen. Not a shirt was to be procured anywhere, and I cheerfully gave him that which I had on my back; so that I was obliged to go without one myself for near three days. Several times during the stay of the French I had assisted in extinguishing fires: even the presence of Marshal Ney was not sufficient to make the French in our houses at all careful in the use of fire. Those thoughtless fellows took the first combustible that fell into their hands, and lighted themselves about with it in every corner. They ran with burning wisps of straw among large piles of trusses, and this was often done in the house where the marshal lay, without its being possible to prevent the practice. A French aid-de-camp, in my presence, took fifty *segars* out of my bureau, just at the moment when I was too busy to hinder him. Whether he likewise helped himself to some fine cravats which lay near them, and which I afterwards missed, I will not pretend to say.

I have suffered a little, you see; but yet I have fortunately escaped the thousands of dangers in which I was incessantly involved. Never while I live shall I forget those days. That same divine Providence which was so manifestly displayed in that arduous conflict, and which crowned the efforts of the powers allied in a sacred cause with so glorious and so signal a victory, evidently extended its care to me. After the battle of Jena, in 1806, Napoleon declared in our city that Leipzig was the most dangerous of his enemies. Little did he imagine that it would once prove so in a very different sense from that which he attached to those words. Here the arm of the Most High arrested his victorious career, of which no mortal eye could have foreseen the termination. I would not exchange the glory—which I may justly assume—the glory of having saved the property of my worthy employer, as far as lay in my power, during those tremendous days of havoc and devastation, for the laurel wreath with which French adulation attempts most unseasonably to entwine the brow of the imperial commander, on account of the battle of Leipzig.

Characteristic Anecdotes

That Napoleon was not quite so much master of himself, during the retreat through Leipzig, as might have been supposed from his countenance, may be inferred from various circumstances. While riding slowly through Peter's gate he was bathed in sweat, and pursued his way towards the very quarter by which the enemy was advancing. It was not till he had gone a considerable distance that he bethought himself, and immediately turned about. He inquired if there was any cross-road to Borna and Altenburg; and, being answered in the negative, he took the way to the Ranstädt gate.

* * * * * * * *

None of the French officers or soldiers could be brought to admit that they had sustained any material loss from the Russian arms in 1812; they maintained, on the contrary, that famine and cold alone had destroyed their legions, and that it was impossible for a French army to be beaten. What excuse will they now have to make, when they return, without baggage and artillery, to their countrymen beyond the Rhine?

* * * * * * * *

That the French prophesied nothing good of their retreat the evening before it commenced, is evinced by the circumstance of their having broken up a great number of gun-carriages, and buried the cannon, or thrown them into marshes or ponds. These yet continue to be daily discovered, and that in places contiguous to houses which are fully inhabited. It is rather singular that they were not observed while engaged in this business, which must certainly have been performed with uncommon silence and expedition.

* * * * * * * *

A Russian officer, to whom complaints were made respecting same irregularities committed by the Cossacks in the villages, expressed himself in the following manner in regard to those troops:

"The officers would gladly put a stop to such proceedings, which are strictly prohibited, and severely punished;—but how is it possible for them to have these men continually under their eye? The nature of the warfare in which they are engaged, which obliges them to be constantly making extensive excursions, prevents this. We are often under the necessity of leaving them for several days together to themselves, that they may explore every wood, every corner, and fatigue and harass the enemy. In services on which no other kind of troops can be employed, they are frequently obliged to struggle alone for several days through every species of hardship and danger; and then, indeed, it is no wonder if they occasionally indulge themselves. On account of the important service which they render to the army, we cannot possibly dispense with them. The incessant vigilance of the Cossacks, who are everywhere at once, renders it extremely difficult for the enemy to reconnoitre, and scarcely possible for him to surprise us; and so much the more frequently are we enabled by them to take him at unawares. In a word, the Cossacks are the eye of the army;—and it is a pity only that it sometimes sees too clearly where it needs not see at all."

116

Memorial

In behalf of the inhabitants of the adjacent villages and hamlets, who have been reduced to extreme distress by the military operations in October, 1813.

The prosperity of Leipzig depends upon commerce, as that of commerce depends upon liberty. Till 1806 it was a flourishing city. With England in particular, whose manufactures and colonial produce were allowed to be freely imported, its commercial relations were of the highest importance. For the opulence which Leipzig then enjoyed it was indebted to its extensive traffic, which contributed to the prosperity of Saxony in general; but it was more particularly the numerous adjacent villages and hamlets that owed to our city their respectability, their improvements, and the easy circumstances of their inhabitants.

The well-known events in October, 1806, rendered Saxony—the then happy Saxony—dependent on the will of Napoleon. Commerce, and the liberty of trade, were annihilated as by magic. A new code was enforced, and Leipzig was severely punished for the traffic which it had heretofore carried on with England and which had been encouraged by its sovereign, as for a heinous crime. Since that catastrophe Saxony had suffered severely, its prosperity had greatly declined, and our city in particular had, in addition to the general burdens, the most grievous oppressions of every kind to endure. How often did Leipzig resemble a military parade or hospital rather than a commercial city! How many pledges of our affection were snatched from us by the contagious fever spread among us by means of the hospitals!—But with the spring of the present year, with the season which usually fills every tender heart with delight, commenced the most melancholy epoch for our country, as it became the theatre of a war which laid it waste without mercy, and of the most sanguinary engagements. After all the hardships which it had suffered, a lot still more severe awaited Leipzig and its vicinity.

From the commencement of October last the French troops here kept daily increasing, as did also their sick and wounded in a most alarming manner. On the 14th Napoleon arrived with his army in our neighbourhood, and the different corps of the allied powers advanced on all sides. On the 15th commenced all round us a great, a holy conflict, for the liberation and independence of Germany, for the peace of Europe, for the repose of the world—a conflict which, after an engagement of three days, that can scarcely be paralleled in history for obstinacy and duration, and at last extended to our city itself, terminated on the 19th of October, through the superior talents of the generals and the valour of their troops, which vanquished all the resistance of despair, in the most complete and glorious victory. The French still defended themselves in our unfortified town, and would have devoted it to destruction; the allies made themselves masters of it by assault at one o'clock, and spared it. They were received with the loudest acclamations by the inhabitants, whose joy was heightened into transport when they beheld their illustrious deliverers, the two emperors, the King of Prussia, and the Crown-Prince of Sweden, enter the place in triumph. During this engagement the Saxon troops went over to the banners of the allies.

This eventful victory justifies the hope of a speedy peace, founded upon the renewed political system of the balance of power,—an honourable, safe, permanent, and general peace, for which, with all its attendant blessings, Europe will be indebted, under divine providence, to the invincible perseverance of England in the contest with France, to the combined energies of the south and the north, and to the exertions of the allied powers, and of the truly patriotic Germans by whom they were joined.

The battle of Leipzig will be ever memorable in the annals of history. A severe lot has hitherto befallen our city. To the burdens and requisitions of every kind, by which it was overwhelmed, were added the suspension of trade, and the injury sustained by the entire suppression this year of our two principal fairs. Our resources are exhausted, and we have yet here a prodigious number of sick and wounded;—upwards of 30,000 in more than 40 military hospitals, with our own poor and the troops yet stationed here for our protection, to be provided for; besides which numberless just claims for the good cause yet remain to be satisfied. But from misfortune itself we will derive new strength and new courage, and our now unfettered commerce affords us the prospect of a happier futurity. We have lost much; but those days when we ourselves knew the want of provisions, and even of bread—those days of horror, danger, and consternation—are past; we yet live, and our city has been preserved through the favour of Heaven and the generosity of the conquerors.

One subject of affliction lies heavy upon our hearts. Our prosperous days afforded us the felicity of being able to perform in its full extent the duty of beneficence towards the necessitous. We have before our eyes many thousands of the inhabitants of the adjacent villages and hamlets, landed proprietors, farmers, ecclesiastics, schoolmasters, artisans of every description, who, some weeks since, were in circumstances more or less easy, and at least knew no want; but now, without a home, and stripped of their all, are with their families perishing of hunger.

Their fields have gained everlasting celebrity, for there the most signal of victories was won for the good cause; but these fields, so lately a paradise, are now, to the distance of from ten to twelve miles, transformed into a desert. What the industry of many years had acquired was annihilated in a few hours. All around is one wide waste. The numerous villages and hamlets are almost all entirely or partially reduced to ashes; the yet remaining buildings are perforated with balls, in a most ruinous condition, and plundered of everything; the barns, cellars, and lofts, are despoiled, and stores of every kind carried off; the implements of farming and domestic economy, for brewing and distilling—in a word, for every purpose—the gardens, plantations, and fruit-trees—are destroyed; the fuel collected for the winter, the gates, the doors, the floors, the wood-work of every description, were consumed in the watch-fires; the horses were taken away, together with all the other cattle; and many families are deploring the loss of beloved relatives, or are doomed to behold them afflicted with sickness and destitute of relief.

The miserable condition of these deplorable victims to the thirst of conquest, the distress which meets our view whenever we cross our thresholds, no language is capable of describing. The horrid spectacle wounds us to the very soul.

But all these unfortunate creatures look up to Leipzig, formerly the source of their prosperity;—their eloquent looks supplicate our aid; and the pang that wrings our bosoms arises from this consideration, that neither the exhausted means of Leipzig nor those of our ruined country are adequate to afford them that relief and support which may enable them to rebuild their habitations, and to return to the exercise of their respective trades and professions.

All the countries of our continent have been more or less drained by this destructive war. Whither then are these poor people, who have such need of assistance—whither are they to look for relief? Whither but to the sea-girt Albion, whose wooden walls defy every hostile attack,—who has, uninjured, maintained the glorious conflict with France, both by water and by land? Ye free, ye beneficent, ye happy Britons, whose generosity is attested by every page of the annals of suffering humanity—whose soil bus been trodden by no hostile foot—who know not the feelings of the wretch that beholds a foreign master revelling in his habitation,—of you the city of Leipzig implores relief for the inhabitants of the circumjacent villages and hamlets, ruined by the military events in the past month of October. We therefore entreat our patrons and friends in England to open a subscription in their behalf. The boon of charity shall be punctually acknowledged in the public papers, and conscientiously distributed, agreeably to the object for which it was designed, by a committee appointed for the purpose. Those who partake of it will bless their benefactors, and their grateful prayers for them will ascend to Heaven.

(Signed)

Frege and Co.

Reichenbach and Co.

Johann Heinrich Küstner and Co.

Leipzig

November 1, 1813

* * * * * * * *

We, the burgomaster and council of the city of Leipzig, hereby attest the truth of the deplorable state of our
city, and of the villages around it, as faithfully and pathetically described in a memorial dated November 1st, and addressed to the British nation by some of our most reputable
and highly-respected fellow-citizens, namely, the bankers
Messrs. Frege and Co. Messrs. Küstner and Co. Messrs. Reichenbach and Co.; and recommend it to the generosity
which has, in all ages, marked the character of the British
nation. We have formally authenticated this attestation, by
affixing to it the seal of our city, and our usual signature.

D. Friedrich Huldreich Carl Siegmann
Acting Burgomaster
Leipzig
November 18, 1813

Fund Raising

FORMED JANUARY, 1814 FOR RELIEVING
THE DISTRESS IN GERMANY

About eight years ago the calamities, occasioned by the
war in different provinces of Germany, gave rise to a subscription and the formation of a committee in London, to
relieve the distresses on the Continent. By the generosity
of the British Public, and with the aid of several respectable Foreigners resident in this country, the sum of nearly
50,000*l.* was remitted to the Continent, which rescued
multitudes of individuals and families from the extremity
of distress, and the very brink of ruin. The committee received, both from Germany and Sweden, the most satisfactory documents, testifying that the various sums transmitted had been received and conscientiously distributed; but
at no period since the existence of this committee has the
mass of every kind of misery been so great, in the country to which their attention was first directed. Never has
the cry of the distressed Germans for help been so urgent,
their appeal to British benevolence so pressing, as at the
present moment. Who could read the reports of the dreadful conflicts which have taken place in Germany, during
the last eventful year; of the many sanguinary battles fought
in Silesia, Lusatia, Bohemia, Saxony, Brandenburg, and oth-

er parts; and peruse the melancholy details of sufferings, almost unexampled in the annals of history, without the most lively emotions? Who could hear of so many thousands of families barbarously driven from Hamburg, in the midst of a severe winter; of so many villages burnt, cities pillaged, whole principalities desolated, and not glow with ardent desire to assist in relieving distress so multifarious and extensive? *To the alleviation of sufferings so dreadful; to the rescue of our fellow-men, who are literally ready to perish: the views of the committee are exclusively directed.* Many well-authenticated afflicting details of the present distress having been, on the 14th Jan. 1814, laid before the committee, it was immediately resolved, in reliance on the liberality of the British public, to remit, by that post, the sum of *three thousand five hundred pounds*, to respectable persons, with directions to form committees of distribution at the several places following:

1. To Leipsic and its vicinity, £500

2. To Dresden and its vicinity, £500

3. To Bautzen and its vicinity, £500

4. To Silesia; on the borders of which, seventy-two villages were almost entirely destroyed, £500

5. To Lauenburg, Luneburg, and the vicinity of Harburg in Hanover, £500

6. To the many thousands who have been forced from their habitations in Hamburg, £1000

   At subsequent meetings the following sums were voted:

7. January 18th, to Erfurt, Naumburg, and their vicinity, £500

8. January 23rd, to Hamburg and its vicinity, £1000

9. To Berlin, its vicinity, and hospitals, £1000

10. To Leipsic and its vicinity, £1000

11. To Silesia and Lusatia, £1000

12. For several hundred children, turned out of the Foundling Hospital at Hamburg, £300

13. January 31st, to Wittemberg and its vicinity, £500

14. To Halle and its vicinity, £500

15. To Dresden and its vicinity, £500

16. To the towns, villages, and hamlets, between Leipsic and Dresden, £1000

17. February 1st, to Hanover and its vicinity, £500

18. To Stettin and its vicinity, £500

19. February 3rd, to Stargard, its hospitals, and vicinity, £300

20. February 10th, to Liegnitz, Neusaltz, Jauer, Buntzlau, and the 72 villages, which are almost entirely destroyed, £2000

21. To Bautzen, with the recommendation of Bischoffswerda, Zittau, Lauban, Loban, and vicinity, £600

22. To Culm and neighbourhood, £500

23. To Dresden and vicinity, £500

24. To Pirna, Freiberg, and vicinity, £500

25. To Lützen and vicinity, £300

26. For the unfortunate peasantry in the vicinity of Leipzig, £1000

27. To Torgau, £500

28. To Naumburg and vicinity, £500

29. To Weissenfels and vicinity, £500

30. To Erfurt and Eisenach, £500

31. To Dessau and vicinity, £500

32. To Fulda, Hanau, and vicinity, £1000

33. To Schwerin, Rostock, and vicinity, £800

34. To Wismar and vicinity, £200

35. To Frankfurt and vicinity, £500

36. To Lübeck and vicinity, £500

37. To Lauenburg, Ratzeburg, Luneburg, Zelle, Harburg, Stade, and neighbouring villages, £1000

38. To Berlin and Whistock, £1000

39. To be held at Berlin, for the sufferers at Magdeburg, when that fortress shall be evacuated by the enemy, £1000

40. To Stettin, £500

41. To Hamburg, £1000

42. To Bremen, £500

43. To Wurzburg, £500

44. February 17, To Stettin, £500

45. To the Exiles from Hamburg, at Altona, Lübeck, Bremen, and wherever they may be, £3000

46. To Kiel, in Holstein, £500

47. To Leipzig, Chemnitz, and Freyberg, and their vicinity, £2000

48. To Dresden, Pirna, and their vicinity, £2000

Total £36,000

At a General Meeting, convened by the committee for relieving the distress in Germany, and other parts of the Continent, on the 27th of January, at the City of London Tavern, Bishopsgate-street, Henry Thornton, Esq. M.P. in the Chair:

The chairman read a letter from His Royal Highness the Duke of Sussex, stating, that an illness, which had deprived him of his rest the preceding night; totally incapacitated him from the proposed pleasure of presiding at a meeting, the purpose of which was so congenial to his feelings, and in the success of which he avowed his heart to be deeply engaged.

The secretary then read an interesting Memorial from the inhabitants of Leipsic, praying that relief from British benevolence, which former experience had taught them, to confide in.

The following Resolutions were agreed to:

1. That it appears to this meeting that the distress arising out of the ravages of war in Germany, and other parts of the Continent, is inconceivably great, and loudly calls on the British nation for the exercise of its accustomed beneficence.

2. That this general meeting, convened by the committee appointed in the year 1805, for relieving the distresses in Germany and other parts of the Continent, approves most cordially of the object of the committee, and especially of the prompt measures taken at their meetings of the 14th and 18th of January, anticipating the liberality of the British public, and sending immediate succour to the places in greatest need.

3. That an addition to the subscriptions already opened by the committee be now applied for, to meet the relief they have already ordered; and that the committee be desired, without delay, to use its utmost endeavours to procure further contributions, to alleviate, as much as possible, the present unparalleled distress on the Continent.

4. That it be recommended to the committee in the distribution of the funds to observe the strictest impartiality and that the measure of dis-

tress in each place or district do regulate the proportion of relief to be afforded.

5. That the several bankers in the metropolis and the country be, and they are hereby, requested to receive subscriptions for this great object of charity; and that the country bankers be, and they are hereby, requested to remit the amount received, on the first day of March, to Henry Thornton, Esq. Bartholomew-lane, with the names of subscribers, and to continue the same on the first day of each subsequent month.

6. That the clergy of the Church of England, and ministers of all religious denominations, be, and they are hereby, earnestly requested to recommend this important object to their several congregations, and to make public collections in aid of its funds.

7. That all the corporate bodies in the United Kingdom be, and they are hereby, respectfully requested to contribute to this important object.

8. That the most respectful thanks of this meeting are due, and that they be presented, to his Royal Highness the Duke of Sussex, for his condescending and, immediate acquiescence in the request that he would take the chair on this important occasion.

Resolved, that the thanks of this meeting be given to Henry Thornton, Esq. for the zeal and ability evinced in his conduct in the chair.

* * * * * * * *

Veracity of Sources

A sub-committee having been commissioned to examine the documental papers and other sources from which Mr. Ackermann's *Narrative of the Most Remarkable Events in and Near Leipzig, &c.* is compiled, as some insinuations have been thrown out that much of what is therein related is rather exaggerated, and Mr. Ackermann having furnished them with the said papers, they were found to consist of:

1. A pamphlet, printed at Leipzig, entitled, *Leipzig, während der Schreckenstage der Schlachten, im Monat October, 1813; als Beytrag zur Chronik dieser Stadt.* (*Leipzig, During the Terrible Days of the Battles in the Month of October, 1813; Being a Supplement to the History of This City.*)

2. A printed advertisement of a large work, to be accompanied with nine plates, the advertisement itself giving a brief but comprehensive account of the battle of Leipzig.

3. A second advertisement, giving a similar description of these battles in German and French.

4. A Letter from Count Schönfeld to Mr. Ackermann, describing the dreadful condition of the villages in the neighbourhood of Leipzig, especially of those

over which the storm of the battle passed.

5. An official paper, signed by some of the principal bankers and merchants at Leipzig, containing an appeal to the benevolence of the British public, in behalf of the sufferers.

6. An official attestation of the truth of the statement made in the said appeal, signed by the acting burgomaster of Leipzig, with the city seal affixed.

7. Several private letters, entering more or less into the detail.

The sub-committee, having read and considered the chief parts of these several sources of information, were unanimous in their opinion, that far from any exaggeration of facts having been resorted to, in presenting this narrative to the British public, facts have been suppressed under an idea that they might shock the feelings of Englishmen, who, in general, by God's mercy, have so imperfect an idea of the horrors of a campaign, and the unspeakable sufferings occasioned by the presence of contending armies, that, to hear more of the detail contained in the said papers, might destroy the effect of exciting compassion by creating disgust, and doubts of the possibility of the existence of such enormities.

The sub-committee were likewise fully persuaded that the accounts contained in these official and printed papers could not have been published at Leipzig itself, without being acknowledged by all as authentic, as they would otherwise have been liable to the censure of every reader and reviewer; and therefore, comparing them also with various similar accounts, received from other places, they feel no hesitation in expressing their opinion, that the narrative published by Mr. Ackermann is a true and faithful representation of such facts as came within the reporter's own observation.

Rev. Wm. Kuper
Rev. Dr. Schwabe
Rev. C.F. Steinkopff
Rev. C.J. Latrobe
Tuesday, February 8th, 1814

Appendix 6

Charity Committee

The following are the instructions given by the London committee to the committees of distribution on the Continent.

Permit me to inform you, that the London committee for relieving the distresses in Germany, and other parts of the Continent, deeply sympathizing in the distressed situation of your town, (or district,) and anxiously wishing to afford some relief to the suffering inhabitants, have devoted the sum of —— to this purpose in the distribution of which they request your attention to the following points:

1. The express design of this charity is to relieve those who have been plunged into poverty and distress by the recent calamities of the War.

2. In the appropriation of its funds, the strictest impartiality is to be observed.

3. The distribution is to take place with the least possible loss of time.

4. No one family or individual is to receive too large a proportion of this charity. The amount of the loss, and all the circumstances of the persons

to be relieved, are duly to be taken into consideration.

5. For these purposes a committee of distribution is immediately to be formed, consisting of magistrates, clergymen, merchants, and such other persons as are most generally respected for their knowledge, discretion, and integrity. Should a committee be already formed for the disposing of contributions received from other quarters, they are requested to choose from among its members a sub-committee for the management of the sums received from London.

6. This committee is requested to keep an accurate list of every person and family they relieve, as well as the sum allotted to each, and to transmit to the London committee such authentic accounts of the distress still prevailing, together with such particulars relative to the good effects produced by the distribution of the charity, as may prove interesting to the public.

7. Finally, the committee of distribution will have the goodness, at the close of their benevolent labours, to draw up a concise report of the manner in which they have applied the funds entrusted to their care, accompanied with such documents as they may deem necessary, and to send the whole to the London committee.

8. The London committee, considering themselves responsible to the public, whose almoners they are, wish to lay particular stress on a fair, equitable, and impartial distribution of this bounty; and as persons of different ranks, and religious denominations, in Great Britain, have

been the contributors, they anxiously wish that the most distressed, without regard to any religious community, whether Christians or Jews, Protestants or Catholics, may receive their due proportion in the distribution.

9. They now conclude with assurances of their deep interest in the sufferings of their brethren on the Continent; and consider it not only a duty, but a privilege, to administer to their necessities, as far as the kind providence of God, through the instrumentality of the British public, may enable them to dispense.

10. The committee of distribution are requested to appoint a correspondent with the London committees, and to transmit their letters to

R.H. Marten
Luke Howard
Secretaries
At the City of London Tavern
London

ALSO FROM LEONAUR
AVAILABLE IN SOFTCOVER OR HARDCOVER WITH DUST JACKET

CAPTAIN OF THE 95th (Rifles) *by Jonathan Leach*—An officer of Wellington's Sharpshooters during the Peninsular, South of France and Waterloo Campaigns of the Napoleonic Wars.

BUGLER AND OFFICER OF THE RIFLES *by William Green & Harry Smith* With the 95th (Rifles) during the Peninsular & Waterloo Campaigns of the Napoleonic Wars

BAYONETS, BUGLES AND BONNETS *by James 'Thomas' Todd*—Experiences of hard soldiering with the 71st Foot - the Highland Light Infantry - through many battles of the Napoleonic wars including the Peninsular & Waterloo Campaigns

THE ADVENTURES OF A LIGHT DRAGOON *by George Farmer & G.R. Gleig*—A cavalryman during the Peninsular & Waterloo Campaigns, in captivity & at the siege of Bhurtpore, India

THE COMPLEAT RIFLEMAN HARRIS *by Benjamin Harris as told to & transcribed by Captain Henry Curling*—The adventures of a soldier of the 95th (Rifles) during the Peninsular Campaign of the Napoleonic Wars

WITH WELLINGTON'S LIGHT CAVALRY *by William Tomkinson*—The Experiences of an officer of the 16th Light Dragoons in the Peninsular and Waterloo campaigns of the Napoleonic Wars.

SURTEES OF THE RIFLES *by William Surtees*—A Soldier of the 95th (Rifles) in the Peninsular campaign of the Napoleonic Wars.

ENSIGN BELL IN THE PENINSULAR WAR *by George Bell*—The Experiences of a young British Soldier of the 34th Regiment 'The Cumberland Gentlemen' in the Napoleonic wars.

WITH THE LIGHT DIVISION *by John H. Cooke*—The Experiences of an Officer of the 43rd Light Infantry in the Peninsula and South of France During the Napoleonic Wars

NAPOLEON'S IMPERIAL GUARD: FROM MARENGO TO WATERLOO *by J. T. Headley*—This is the story of Napoleon's Imperial Guard from the bearskin caps of the grenadiers to the flamboyance of their mounted chasseurs, their principal characters and the men who commanded them.

BATTLES & SIEGES OF THE PENINSULAR WAR *by W. H. Fitchett*—Corunna, Busaco, Albuera, Ciudad Rodrigo, Badajos, Salamanca, San Sebastian & Others

LEONAUR

ALSO FROM LEONAUR

AVAILABLE IN SOFTCOVER OR HARDCOVER WITH DUST JACKET

WELLINGTON AND THE PYRENEES CAMPAIGN VOLUME I: FROM VITORIA TO THE BIDASSOA by *F. C. Beatson*—The final phase of the campaign in the Iberian Peninsula.

WELLINGTON AND THE INVASION OF FRANCE VOLUME II: THE BIDASSOA TO THE BATTLE OF THE NIVELLE by *F. C. Beatson*—The second of Beatson's series on the fall of Revolutionary France published by Leonaur, the reader is once again taken into the centre of Wellington's strategic and tactical genius.

WELLINGTON AND THE FALL OF FRANCE VOLUME III: THE GAVES AND THE BATTLE OF ORTHEZ by *F. C. Beatson*—This final chapter of F. C. Beatson's brilliant trilogy shows the 'captain of the age' at his most inspired and makes all three books essential additions to any Peninsular War library.

NAVAL BATTLES OF THE NAPOLEONIC WARS by *W. H. Fitchett*—Cape St.Vincent, the Nile, Cadiz, Copenhagen, Trafalgar & Others

SERGEANT GUILLEMARD: THE MAN WHO SHOT NELSON? by *Robert Guillemard*—A Soldier of the Infantry of the French Army of Napoleon on Campaign Throughout Europe

WITH THE GUARDS ACROSS THE PYRENEES by *Robert Batty*—The Experiences of a British Officer of Wellington's Army During the Battles for the Fall of Napoleonic France, 1813.

A STAFF OFFICER IN THE PENINSULA by *E. W. Buckham*—An Officer of the British Staff Corps Cavalry During the Peninsula Campaign of the Napoleonic Wars

THE LEIPZIG CAMPAIGN: 1813—NAPOLEON AND THE "BATTLE OF THE NATIONS" by *F. N. Maude*—Colonel Maude's analysis of Napoleon's campaign of 1813.

BUGEAUD: A PACK WITH A BATON by *Thomas Robert Bugeaud*—The Early Campaigns of a Soldier of Napoleon's Army Who Would Become a Marshal of France.

TWO LEONAUR ORIGINALS

SERGEANT NICOL by *Daniel Nicol*—The Experiences of a Gordon Highlander During the Napoleonic Wars in Egypt, the Peninsula and France.

WATERLOO RECOLLECTIONS by *Frederick Llewellyn*—Rare First Hand Accounts, Letters, Reports and Retellings from the Campaign of 1815.

LEONAUR

ALSO FROM LEONAUR
AVAILABLE IN SOFTCOVER OR HARDCOVER WITH DUST JACKET

A JOURNAL OF THE SECOND SIKH WAR by *Daniel A. Sandford*—The Experiences of an Ensign of the 2nd Bengal European Regiment During the Campaign in the Punjab, India, 1848-49.

LAKE'S CAMPAIGNS IN INDIA by *Hugh Pearse*—The Second Anglo Maratha War, 1803-1807. Often neglected by historians and students alike, Lake's Indian campaign was fought against a resourceful and ruthless enemy-almost always superior in numbers to his own forces.

BRITAIN IN AFGHANISTAN 1: THE FIRST AFGHAN WAR 1839-42 by *Archibald Forbes*—Following over a century of the gradual assumption of sovereignty of the Indian Sub-Continent, the British Empire, in the form of the Honourable East India Company, supported by troops of the new Queen Victoria's army, found itself inevitably at the natural boundaries that surround Afghanistan. There it set in motion a series of disastrous events-the first of which was to march into the country at all.

BRITAIN IN AFGHANISTAN 2: THE SECOND AFGHAN WAR 1878-80 by *Archibald Forbes*—This the history of the Second Afghan War-another episode of British military history typified by savagery, massacre, siege and battles.

UP AMONG THE PANDIES by *Vivian Dering Majendie*—An outstanding account of the campaign for the fall of Lucknow. This is a vital book of war as fought by the British Army of the mid-nineteenth century, but in truth it is also an essential book of war that will enthral.

BLOW THE BUGLE, DRAW THE SWORD by *W. H. G. Kingston*—The Wars, Campaigns, Regiments and Soldiers of the British & Indian Armies During the Victorian Era, 1839-1898.

INDIAN MUTINY 150th ANNIVERSARY: A LEONAUR ORIGINAL

MUTINY: 1857 by *James Humphries*—It is now 150 years since the 'Indian Mutiny' burst like an engulfing flame on the British soldiers, their families and the civilians of the Empire in North East India. The Bengal Native army arose in violent rebellion, and the once peaceful countryside became a battleground as Native sepoys and elements of the Indian population massacred their British masters and defeated them in open battle. As the tide turned, a vengeful army of British and loyal Indian troops repressed the insurgency with a savagery that knew no mercy. It was a time of fear and slaughter. James Humphries has drawn together the voices of those dreadful days for this commemorative book.

Printed in the USA
CPSIA information can be obtained
at www.ICGtesting.com
LVHW090546171123
763818LV00070B/1105/J